Relish
SOUTH EAST

Original recipes from the region's
finest chefs and restaurants.
Introduction by Angela Hartnett, MBE.

First Published 2015
By Relish Publications
Shield Green Farm, Tritlington,
Northumberland, NE61 3DX.
Twitter: @Relish_Cookbook

ISBN: 978-0-9575370-7-1

Publisher: Duncan L Peters
General Manager: Teresa Peters
Design: Vicki Brown
Relish Photography: Andy Richardson
www.awaywithmedia.com Twitter: @andyrichardson1
Editorial Consultant: Paul Robertson
Proofing Coordinator: Valerie McLeod
Sales: Wendy Rutterford
Coordinator: Rebecca Laycock

Front cover photograph by: Andy Richardson

Printed in Poland on behalf of Latitude Press

Relish
PUBLICATIONS

OUR HAND PICKED RESTAURANTS

As the proud owner of a Relish cookbook, you may subscribe for your own personal Relish Rewards card which entitles you to free membership for one year.

You can access the Relish members' area on our website and find out what exclusive offers are available to you from the fantastic restaurants featured in our series of books throughout the UK.

SUBSCRIBE FOR YOUR REWARD CARD ON OUR HOMEPAGE
Simply register your name, address and title of Relish book purchased to receive your **FREE Relish Reward Card** www.relishpublications.co.uk

When you make a reservation, simply let the restaurant know that you are a member and take your card along with you.

WHAT ARE THE REWARDS?
The rewards will continue to be updated on the website so do check and keep in touch. These range from a free bottle of Champagne to free gifts when you dine. Relish will send you a quarterly newsletter with special discounts, rewards and free recipes. We are about quality not quantity!

All offers are subject to change. See the Relish website for details.

www.relishpublications.co.uk

004 CONTENTS

006
CONTENTS

New Forest Wild Mushroom Ragu, Leek, Confit Tomato and Garlic, Fried Quail Egg - **Page 064**

009
STARTERS

011
MAINS

013
DESSERTS

FOREWORD BY ANGELA HARTNETT

I was brought up in Kent with a passion for good, honest food instilled in me by my Italian grandmother and mother. Meals were homely but always made from the best seasonal ingredients we could afford and these experiences have formed my approach as a chef today.

From a young age I knew I wanted to have my own business and, after completing a Modern History degree, I chose to pursue this within the hospitality industry. Gordon Ramsay gave me my first major opportunities and I graduated through Aubergine and L'Oranger, then went on to launch Verre in Dubai, MENU and The Grill Room at The Connaught under his mentorship.

In 2008 I opened my own restaurant, Murano in Mayfair, which was awarded a Michelin Star shortly afterwards. Overseeing the catering at London 2012's Olympic Hospitality Centre was a career highlight and the following year I opened Hartnett Holder & Co at Lime Wood Hotel in Hampshire, in partnership with Robin Hutson and chef Luke Holder. Since then I have opened two more London restaurants, Merchants Tavern in Shoreditch, in collaboration with head chef Neil Borthwick, and Café Murano, a relaxed little sister to Murano, where I create the Northern Italian inspired menu with my head chef Sam Williams.

As you can see, it's all got quite busy! As well as placing trust in dedicated teams, the thread running through all the restaurants I'm involved with is that commitment to seasonal ingredients, treated simply to best bring out their flavour and bring everyone to the dinner table.

The South East of England is home to some incredible produce, from wild mushrooms to garlic, venison, beef and lamb, and Luke and I celebrate all these ingredients in our menus at Hartnett Holder & Co. The producers who farm and rear this produce are an important part of the local community and supporting them helps the community to prosper.

I hope that this book might suggest some enjoyable ideas for making the most of the edible treasures we have on our doorstep; both places to eat them and new, exciting ways to cook them.

Angela Hartnett, MBE

016
BOULTERS
RESTAURANT & BAR

Boulters Lock Island, Maidenhead, Berkshire, SL6 8PE

01628 621 291
www.boultersrestaurant.co.uk

Located on the edge of Boulters Lock Island with views down the River Thames, Boulters Restaurant & Bar is truly blessed with a fantastic location.

This however, tells only half the story, as head chef Daniel Woodhouse and his team work all the harder to provide food and service to complement the beautiful panorama.

Bought by the Dennis family in 2008, Boulters was fully refurbished and opened in 2009, much to the pleasure of the locals.

Chef Woodhouse leads a talented, youthful team who create unique and eclectic food, based on local produce. "We favour a simple marriage of flavours and sound cooking techniques," says Woodhouse. His efforts have secured two Rosettes in the AA guide during the past two years.

Originally from Newcastle upon Tyne, Woodhouse worked in London for many years for some of the best chefs in Britain, before leaving to find his own style of cooking.

Coming from an artistic background, Woodhouse cooks food in the brasserie that is a mixture of modern and classic, simple and not so simple. He adds, "In the final analysis, only one thing matters - it's all about flavour."

Relish Restaurant Rewards
See page 003 for details.

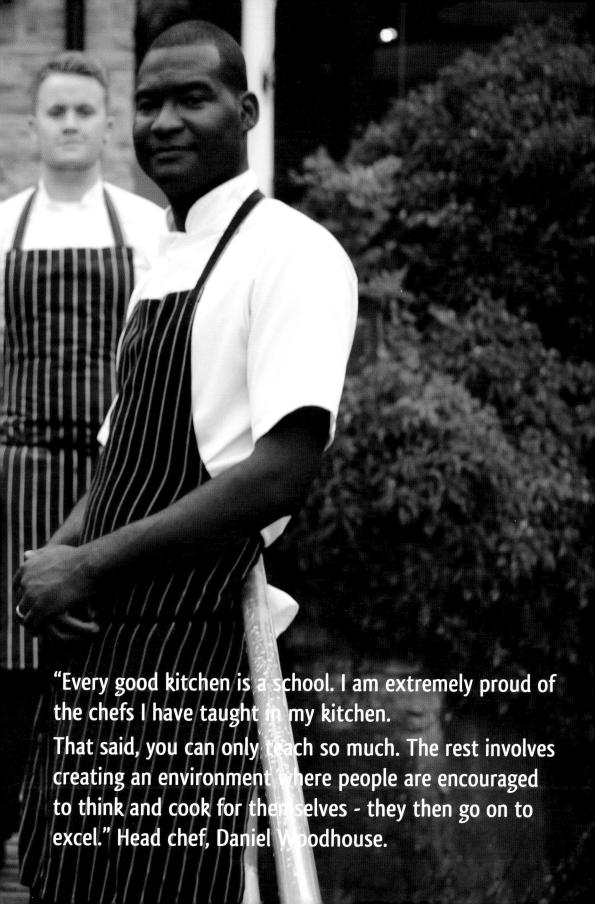

"Every good kitchen is a school. I am extremely proud of the chefs I have taught in my kitchen.

That said, you can only teach so much. The rest involves creating an environment where people are encouraged to think and cook for themselves - they then go on to excel." Head chef, Daniel Woodhouse.

ROAST LOCAL WOOD PIGEON, ORANGE & WATERCRESS SALAD, HAZELNUTS, SAUCE BIGARADE

SERVES 4

Kanu KCB Chenin Blanc
(South Africa)

Ingredients

Pigeon

4 oven ready pigeons
2 cloves garlic
2 sprigs thyme
1 tbsp coriander seeds
oil or butter (to *confit*)

Sauce Bigarade

½ lemon (juice and zest of)
2 oranges (juice and zest of)
25g caster sugar
2 tbsp red wine vinegar
400ml veal stock
parsley (chopped)
butter (knob of)

Watercress Purée

200g watercress
100g spinach
200ml double cream (boiled)
salt and pepper

To Serve

100g hazelnuts (toasted, crushed)
1 punnet micro watercress
2 large oranges (segmented)

Method

For The Pigeon

Preheat the oven to180°C (fan).

Blow torch the pigeons, discarding any small feathers and caramelising the flesh, rendering down the fat and starting the *Maillard reaction.*

Remove the breasts and reserve.

Take the legs off and place them in an ovenproof dish. Cover with butter or oil, adding in the garlic, thyme and coriander seeds. Slowly *confit* for 2-3 hours until very tender.

> **Chef's Tip**
>
> This dish can be replicated with partridge if you can't get hold of wood pigeon.

For The Sauce Bigarade

Julienne the citrus zest then *blanch* it 3 times. Set aside.

Put the sugar in a pan and caramelise. Add the vinegar, then the citrus juice and reduce to a glaze. Pour in the veal stock and reduce to a sauce consistency, adding the zest for the last 5 minutes. Season with a little salt and pepper. Stir through a knob of butter and parsley to finish.

For The Watercress Purée

Blanch the vegetables in boiling water for 2 minutes, then submerge into iced water. Squeeze out the water, place in a blender, add the cream, blend and pass through a sieve. Season with salt and pepper.

To Serve

Pan fry the pigeon breasts in a hot pan for 2-4 minutes on each side. Heat the legs then arrange on the plate with the breasts. Pour the sauce over the meat and a little around the plate. Sprinkle with the hazelnuts. Garnish with a swipe of watercress purée, fresh watercress and orange segments.

ROAST FILLET & BRAISED OXTAIL OF BERKSHIRE BEEF, ENGLISH PEA RISOTTO & TOMATO FONDUE

SERVES 4

 Margaux Brio 2009
(France)

Ingredients

Beef Fillet

500g Berkshire beef fillet
1 tbsp Dijon mustard
2 tbsp chopped herbs (of your choice)

Oxtail

300g oxtail (seasoned)
500ml beef stock
2 sprigs thyme
butter (knob of), 2 tbsp oil
2 carrots (diced), 1 onion (diced)
1 stick celery (diced)
1 bay leaf, 2 cloves garlic
1 egg (beaten), plain flour (to dust)
panko breadcrumbs (to coat)

Pea Risotto

1 banana shallot (chopped)
100g butter
250g risotto rice (Vialoni Nano)
salt (pinch of)
188ml white wine, 188ml vegetable stock
50g Parmesan (grated), 50g mascarpone
extra vegetable stock (to loosen)
200g fresh peas (*blanched*)

Tomato Fondue

10 plum tomatoes
salt (pinch of), sugar (pinch of)
white balsamic (drizzle of)
1 clove garlic (crushed), 1 sprig thyme (picked)

Pea Purée

300g peas (podded), 200ml double cream
1 tsp sugar, salt and pepper

To Serve

1 punnet fresh pea shoots
1 tomato (flesh only, diced)

Method

For The Oxtail (Prepare ahead)

Seal the oxtail in a pan with a little oil, butter and 1 sprig of thyme. Cover with the beef stock. In a separate pan, roast off the diced vegetables and, when softened, add to the oxtail. Add the remaining thyme, bay leaf and garlic. Simmer gently for 1-2 hours until tender and falling off the bone.

Season and bind the meat together in small balls. Chill before rolling in the flour and beaten egg. Finally, coat in breadcrumbs.

For The Pea Risotto

Sweat the shallot in the butter, add the rice and stir for another minute. Add a pinch of salt, then slowly add the white wine, followed by the stock, stirring continuously. When all the liquid has gone, pour onto a tray and set aside.

For The Tomato Fondue

Preheat the oven to 80°C (fan).

Remove the skin and seeds from the tomatoes. Place the tomato flesh on a tray with a little salt, sugar and white balsamic. Scatter with the garlic and thyme leaves. Cook in the oven for 2 hours. Purée in a food processor until it forms a paste.

For The Pea Purée

Season a pan of boiling water with salt and sugar. *Blanch* the peas for 2 minutes until soft. Separately boil the double cream, blend with the peas and pass through a sieve. Season to taste.

To Serve

Preheat the oven to 180°C (fan).

Roast the beef to your own preference, brush with Dijon mustard, then roll in chopped herbs. Cook out the risotto with more vegetable stock, the mascarpone, grated Parmesan and the peas.

Deep fry the oxtail balls at 190°C for 3-4 minutes. Assemble as per the photograph, garnishing with the pea shoots and a *quenelle* of the tomato fondue.

> **Chef's Tip**
>
> Only try this dish between May and September when English peas are in season.

NEAPOLITAN WITH RASPBERRY ICE CREAM

SERVES 4

 Buitenverwachting Dessert Wine (South Africa)

Ingredients

Crème Anglaise
100g sugar
6 egg yolks, 200ml milk
200ml double cream
3 leaves gelatine (soaked)

Raspberry Ice Cream
500g raspberry purée
360g caster sugar
400ml double cream
160g egg yolks (from 8-9 eggs)

Raspberry Mousse
200ml double cream (semi-whipped)
200g raspberry purée
100ml Crème Anglaise

Vanilla Panna Cotta
400ml double cream, 100ml full-fat milk
80g sugar
2½ leaves silver leaf gelatine (soaked)
1 vanilla pod (scraped)

Chocolate Mousse
285g 64% chocolate
398ml Crème Anglaise
228ml double cream (semi-whipped)

Tuile
100g sugar, 100ml water
½ vanilla pod
1 pack Feuille de Brick pastry

Sauce Mousseline
2 egg yolks (45g), 200g sugar
200ml water
½ vanilla pod

Crumble Mix
100g sugar
100g butter (very soft)
200g plain flour

Garnish
fresh raspberries, raspberry purée

3 mousse moulds (15cm x 15cm)

Method

To Make The Crème Anglaise (Make first)
Whisk the sugar and egg yolks together until light and fluffy. Heat the milk and cream together, then slowly add to the egg mix whilst whisking continuously. Stir in the softened gelatine.

For The Raspberry Ice Cream (Make the day before)
Blitz the purée and 200g of sugar together in a blender. Whisk the remaining sugar and the egg yolks in a machine for 10-15 minutes, to make a *sabayon*. Gently fold the fruit into the *sabayon*. In a separate bowl, semi-whip the double cream, then fold in the fruit *sabayon*. Place into a clean, dry, lidded plastic container and transfer to the freezer. Wait until the next day to eat it (if you can).

For The Raspberry Mousse (Make the day before)
Add the purée to the Crème Anglaise, then fold in the double cream. Pour into the mousse mould and freeze overnight.

For The Vanilla Panna Cotta
Bring the cream, milk, sugar and vanilla to the boil. Stir in the gelatine, then chill over ice before setting in a mousse mould in the fridge for 3 hours.

For The Chocolate Mousse
Gently melt the chocolate in the Crème Anglaise. When it cools to room temperature, fold in the cream and set in the mousse mould in the fridge for 2 hours.

For The Tuile
Boil the sugar, water and vanilla together. Leave to cool.
Cut the pastry into strips, 14cm x 5cm. Place on a non-stick mat, brush with the syrup, then place another mat on top. Bake at 150°C (fan) for 10-15 minutes until golden.

For The Sauce Mousseline
Start by whisking the egg yolks. Meanwhile, bring the sugar, vanilla and water together in a pan to 121°C. Pour onto the egg yolks and keep whisking until at room temperature and they are light and fluffy.

For The Crumble Mix
Combine all the ingredients, using a beater attachment, until it forms a breadcrumb texture.
Scatter thinly on a lined, shallow tray. Bake at 150°C (fan) until golden brown - about 15 minutes.

To Serve
Place the raspberry mousse, vanilla panna cotta and chocolate mousse all on top of each other. Slice into wedges and sandwich between the pastry tuiles. Dress the plate with sauce mousseline, then burn with a blow torch. Place the sandwich, some raspberries and finally a *quenelle* of the ice cream on top of the crumble mix.

BUCKINGHAMSHIRE, THE BEAUTIFUL SOUTH

Chris Wheeler, Executive Chef, Humphry's, Stoke Park Country Club, Spa & Hotel

Buckinghamshire is a beautiful county, which I am blessed to have worked in for the past 11 years. Throughout the county, there are so many places to visit and beautiful countryside to enjoy. Buckinghamshire is unique in the fact that it has the most National Trust properties in the country, is the Birthplace of the Paralympic Movement, is home to ITV's Midsomer Murders and Roald Dahl, the children's author, who is celebrated at two museums.

The Stoke Park estate, where I work, has an incredible history. It dates back more than 1,000 years and has belonged to important figures in history such as Queen Elizabeth I, Sir Edward Coke (First Lord Chief Justice of England who prosecuted Guy Fawkes and the Gunpowder Plotters, and famously coined the phrase 'An Englishman's Home is his Castle') and the Penn family, the founding fathers of Pennsylvania. It was John Penn (1760-1834), a soldier, scholar and poet, who was responsible for most of what can still be seen at the estate today. The estate was used as a private residence until 1908. Nick "Pa" Lane Jackson, founder of The Corinthians, purchased the estate and created

Stoke Park, Britain's first Country Club. Stoke Park has also featured in many movies, such as James Bond's 'Goldfinger', Layer Cake and Bridget Jones's Diary.

Stoke Park is still a country club today and also a luxury 5 AA Red star hotel. Stoke Park hosts the annual pre-Wimbledon tennis tournament, The Boodles, which sees the world's top tennis stars come to the county. It is also still family owned and operated by a Buckinghamshire based family.

At Stoke Park we always support local causes and businesses. In Humphry's most of my ingredients are locally sourced from farms and nurseries, such as Pinewood Nurseries and Tim's Dairy. Buckinghamshire is also well known for asparagus and I go out each year picking asparagus from Copas Farm with my twin daughters, Vittoria and Vanessa. We are so fortunate to have amazing restaurants as well throughout the county. We are very proud to be in Buckinghamshire and to be a part of Relish South East, a truly exquisite collection of delicious recipes.

028
HUMPHRY'S

Stoke Park Country Club, Spa & Hotel, Park Road, Stoke Poges, Buckinghamshire, SL2 4PG

01753 71 71 71
www.stokepark.com Twitter: @StokePark @HumphrysSP

Paralleling Stoke Park's illustrious past is the culinary excellence of executive chef, Chris Wheeler, who celebrated his eleventh year at Stoke Park in 2014. Stoke Park's fine dining restaurant, Humphry's (previously The Dining Room) launched in 2010 and was instantly awarded two AA Rosettes. After rebranding in 2012 to Humphry's, the restaurant was awarded its third AA Rosette in January 2013.

The name Humphry's originates from the famous British landscape designer Humphry Repton. In the 1790s, Humphry Repton created some of the main features of the magnificent landscape at Stoke Park. In particular, he designed the beautiful bridge that you can see from the restaurant.

Humphry's is a stunning, light-filled restaurant featuring panoramic views of the bridge, estate and the lake, offering both à la carte and table d'hôte menus available for lunch, as well as a three course dinner menu and seven course tasting menu.

Before arriving to Stoke Park, Chris had worked in Michelin starred kitchens under Jean-Christophe Novelli as his Group Head Chef. He worked at Le Provence, Lymington, Four Seasons, Park Lane, Maison Novelli and Les Saveurs, Mayfair. He appeared in the TV programme Hell's Kitchen 2 alongside Jean-Christophe in 2005.

Chris joined Stoke Park in 2003 and for the past 11 years he has steadily built Stoke Park's culinary reputation. In addition to the 3 AA Rosettes, much praise and accolades have been attributed to Chris and his team, with Woman and Home magazine recently stating, 'Humphry's is the last word in fine dining' and The Daily Telegraph naming Stoke Park as having one of 'Britain's Best Afternoon Teas'. Humphry's was voted in the 'Top 20 Best Out of Town Restaurants' by Harper's Bazaar, 'Top 5 Out of Town Restaurants' by the Square Meal Restaurant Guide, won 'Best Local Menu' for its use of local produce at the Buckinghamshire and Berkshire Life Food and Drink Awards, and featured in Tatler's Restaurant Guide 2013 and again in 2014, with the editor writing that Chris had cooked two of the best dishes he had ever had!

Relish Restaurant Rewards
See page 003 for details.

The menu at Humphry's offers modern British cuisine with a twist.

In 2014 Chris has cooked up a storm on both BBC1's Saturday Kitchen and Channel 4's Sunday Brunch!

QUAIL, CHICKEN & PISTACHIO TERRINE, PICKLED SHIMEJI MUSHROOM, MADEIRA JELLY

SERVES 4

 Morgon, Château de Raousset, 2012 (France)

Ingredients

Pickled Shimeji Mushroom

80ml white wine vinegar
55g sugar
200ml water
5 peppercorns
1 pack Shimeji mushrooms
2 sprigs thyme
2 sprigs rosemary
1 clove garlic (chopped)
1 shallot (chopped)

Madeira Jelly

300ml Madeira wine
3 leaves bronze gelatine (softened)

Chicken And Pistachio Terrine

2 oven ready quails
2 chicken legs
5 sprigs thyme
2 sprigs rosemary
1 clove garlic
5 peppercorns
1 bay leaf
500ml vegetable oil
100g peeled pistachios
1 packet pancetta

To Serve

10g Sel de Rose salt (pink)
pain Poilâne crisp

terrine mould (lined with cling film)

Method

For The Pickled Shimeji Mushrooms

Create the pickling *liquor* by bringing the vinegar, sugar, water and peppercorns to the boil. Slowly pan fry the Shimeji mushrooms with the herbs, garlic and shallot. Once lightly cooked, add the pickling *liquor* and allow to cool.

For The Madeira Jelly

Bring the Madeira to the boil. Squeeze out any excess water from the gelatine and add it to the Madeira. Whisk and remove from the heat. Pass through a sieve into a suitable container to set for 1 hour.

For The Terrine

Preheat the oven to 150°C.

Confit the quails and chicken legs by placing them in an oven proof container and covering them with the vegetable oil.
Add the thyme, rosemary, garlic, bay leaf and peppercorns, then cover with baking paper and tin foil. Slow cook the birds in the oven for 2-2½ hours depending on size.

Remove the quails and chicken from the oven. Remove from the oil and allow to cool slightly. Once the meat is at a warm temperature, pick the meat from the bone, remove the skin and any excess cartilage.

In a food processor, blend the pistachios to a coarse dust. Separate the picked meat into 3 equal amounts and add salt and pepper as required. Press the first layer into your mould and press firmly, ensuring the layer is level, then sprinkle the pistachios to completely cover the meat. Repeat this process twice, pressing firmly between each layer.

Set your terrine in the fridge until firm for 1 hour. Once cold, trim, wrap in pancetta and cling film. Steam for 7 minutes and cool. Slice as required.

Chef's Tip

Make sure that you pick the quail and chicken meat from the bone whilst still warm and make the terrine straight away. Try not to let the meat cool too much.

To Serve

Sprinkle Sel de Rose across the plate and cut the Madeira jelly into ½cm dice. Drain the Shimeji mushrooms and scatter around the terrine. Garnish with the pain Poilâne crisp.

PAN FRIED PAVE OF HALIBUT WITH A BUTTERNUT SQUASH, PEA & BASIL RISOTTO & CRISPY LEEK

SERVES 4

 Chapel Down, Bacchus, Reserve, 2011
(Kent, England)

Ingredients

Butternut Squash

1 butternut squash (washed)
olive oil
2 cloves garlic (peeled, sliced)
2 sprigs fresh rosemary

Pea And Basil Risotto

1 shallot (peeled, finely chopped)
1 large leek (well rinsed, trimmed, finely chopped)
150g risotto rice
salt and freshly ground black pepper
8 tbsp white wine
250ml hot vegetable stock
150g fresh peas
20g butter (diced)
100g Parmesan (grated)
2 tsp mascarpone
few fresh basil leaves (chopped)

Pave Of Halibut

4 x 125g halibut fillets
1 onion (peeled, finely chopped)
1 stick celery (trimmed, diced)
100ml fish stock
25ml double cream
chopped chives (handful of)
4 marinated artichokes
1 chopped tomato (*concasse*)

Garnish

crispy fried leeks
chive cress

Method

For The Butternut Squash

Preheat the oven to 180°C.

Peel the squash and remove the seeds. Discard the skin and seeds. Cut the flesh into 1cm dice, reserve the trimmings. Arrange the dice on a roasting tray, drizzle over a little olive oil and sprinkle over the garlic and rosemary. Roast in the oven until the butternut squash is soft. Blend half the baked squash, then season (for the sauce).

For The Risotto

Heat a little oil in a pan, add the shallot and leek. Sweat until softened. Stir in the rice and season. Add half the wine, and slowly add the hot stock, a ladleful at a time, until the risotto is just cooked.

Add the fresh peas, the remaining half of the roasted squash and stir carefully. Fold in the butter, grated Parmesan, mascarpone and basil. Check the seasoning.

> **Chef's Tip**
>
> Make sure you take the risotto off the heat, then add the Parmesan and serve immediately. Do not return to the heat after you've added the Parmesan.

For The Pave Of Halibut

Preheat the oven to 180°C.

Heat a little olive oil in a small pan. Sweat the onion, celery and butternut squash trimmings, then add the remaining white wine and cook until it has reduced by half.

Add the fish stock, reduce again by half, add the cream, season and simmer for 5 minutes. Blend until smooth, season, then stir in the chives and chopped tomato.

Cut the artichokes in half lengthways and roast in the oven until golden brown. Season the halibut and pan fry on both sides until golden brown. Transfer to a non-stick baking tray and cook in the oven for 5 minutes.

To Serve

Place a portion of butternut squash purée on each place, using a metal ring mould to give a perfect shape, then top with a portion of risotto. Add a halibut fillet on top, then arrange 2 artichoke halves. Spoon the sauce around the halibut and garnish with some crispy leek and chive cress.

ENGLISH RASPBERRY SOUFFLE WITH CHEESECAKE ICE CREAM & RASPBERRY SAUCE

SERVES 4

 Côteaux Du Layon, Chaume, Loire Valley, Domaine des Forges, 2011 (France)

Ingredients

Raspberry Soufflé Base

125g raspberry purée
250g caster sugar
9g cornflour
15ml Chambord raspberry liqueur

Soufflé

150g raspberry soufflé base (see above)
100g egg whites (from about 3 eggs)
35g caster sugar

Cheesecake Ice Cream

200ml milk
100g caster sugar
300g cream cheese

Biscuit Base

150g digestive biscuits
75g butter (melted)

Raspberry Sauce

2 punnets fresh raspberries
¼ lemon (juice of)
50g caster sugar

Dehydrated Raspberry Tuile

125g raspberry purée
25g caster sugar

4 ramekins

Chef's Tip
Make sure you fold the soufflé mixture - do not whip it.

Method

For Raspberry Soufflé Base (Prepare in advance)
Place the raspberry purée into a pan with the sugar and bring to the boil. Mix the Chambord and cornflour together. Once the purée has started to boil, mix in the cornflour mixture and cook for 1 minute. Once thickened, leave to cool. Cover the top with cling film so that it doesn't get a crust. Next, soften some butter and, using a pastry brush, grease your ramekin in a bottom to top motion evenly around all the edges. Pour in some caster sugar and roll it around the ramekin. Empty the excess sugar out and place the ramekins into the fridge.

For The Cheesecake Ice Cream
Place the milk and sugar into a pan and bring to the boil. Slowly pour onto the cream cheese and whisk until smooth. Place into the freezer and beat each hour with a wooden spoon until frozen and smooth. (Alternatively, churn in an ice cream machine).

For The Biscuit Base
Crush the digestive biscuits and combine with the melted butter.

For The Raspberry Sauce
Using a hand blender, blitz the raspberries and lemon together and pass through a *chinois*. Pour into a pan, add the sugar and bring to the boil.

For The Dehydrated Raspberry Tuile (Prepare in advance)
Preheat the oven to 95ºC.
Place all ingredients into a pan and reduce by half. Cool in the fridge. Once cooled, spread evenly, using a palette knife, over greaseproof paper. Place into the oven for 8 hours to crispen up.

For The Soufflé
Preheat the oven to 190ºC.
Weigh out 150g of the raspberry soufflé base.
In a clean bowl, whisk the egg whites to a soft peak. Slowly add the caster sugar and whisk for 1 minute. Fold the egg white into the soufflé base until fully incorporated.
Pipe into the ramekins and bake in the oven for 10 minutes. Serve immediately!

To Serve
Place a small amount of the biscuit base on the plate. Finish with one scoop of ice cream on top. Arrange the cooked soufflé next to it and serve with warm raspberry sauce on the side. Garnish with the tuile.

HAMPSHIRE, THE KITCHEN PANTRY

Matthew Tomkinson, Head Chef, The Terrace at The Montagu Arms

Growing up in the north west of England, Hampshire appeared to my younger self as remote a destination as the outer reaches of Scotland; I certainly didn't envisage it as a place I'd lay down roots. Yet here I am, seven years on in my adopted county, and I can honestly say I wouldn't choose to live anywhere else.

A big part of the appeal, as a chef, is the produce we have on offer here. If Kent is the garden of England, Hampshire is surely the kitchen pantry. The shellfish, wild sea bass and oysters that can be found in our coastal waters are better than any I've sampled elsewhere, while the New Forest woodlands that surround the Montagu Arms serve as rearing grounds for some of the UK's tastiest free-range beef and pork.

Those whose palates veer on the wild side will delight in the foraging to be had in this beautiful county. Of the 12,000 species of fungi that grow across Britain, nearly a quarter can be found in the New Forest alone - with local ceps, girolles and morels regularly making an appearance on my menus.

Head inland to Alresford, meanwhile, and you'll discover one of our best kept secrets: the home of watercress. The chalky streams that border this pastel coloured Georgian town, seven miles north east of Winchester, provide the perfect environment for cultivating the peppery salad leaf. There's even an annual festival held in its honour every May.

It's exciting, local produce such as this that has motivated me to build a home in Hampshire - that and the rich pickings of restaurants and pubs sprinkled across the county, which I'm always keen to seek out and enjoy.

Relish South East has brought together some of the most talented chefs from these establishments to showcase our region's culinary credentials. So prepare to be inspired as you browse the following pages. The recipes you'll find here will genuinely give you food for thought!

040
HARTNETT HOLDER & CO

Lime Wood, Beaulieu Road, Lyndhurst, Hampshire, SO43 7FZ

02380 287 177
www.limewoodhotel.co.uk/hartnett-holder-and-co Twitter: @hhandco

Lime Wood is the UK's most talked about hotel. Set in the midst of the beautiful New Forest National Park, just an hour and a half from London, it is the perfect escape for a midweek or weekend getaway. After five years in the making, Lime Wood is a luxury country house hotel with a difference. Designed by Charles Morris and Ben Pentreath, with interiors added by David Collins and more recently Martin Brudnizki, it has kept the spirit of the past whilst maintaining a contemporary twist.

The food scene at Lime Wood is in a league of its own. The award-winning Hartnett Holder & Co creates sublime dishes using local, organic produce and forest food from their doorstep including; wild mushrooms, garlic, local venison and home-reared beef and lamb. Head chef Luke Holder and Michelin-starred chef Angela Hartnett serve up their concept of 'fun dining' in a creative British style with an Italian pedigree served in a truly idyllic setting. Luke has worked in some of London's busiest and most exclusive restaurants including Orrery and the Oxo Tower. He then spent a year cooking in the Italian kitchen of 3 Michelin starred Enoteca Pinchiorri in Florence. During this time he changed his philosophy of food, firmly placing his focus on cooking locally and seasonally, at the highest level. As a founding partner of Lime Wood's restaurant Hartnett Holder & Co, Luke's relaxed style is comfortable and upscale at the same time. His partner in the kitchen, co-head chef Angela Hartnett and their team create locally sourced English dishes with flare, which salutes their joint Italian culinary backgrounds. His approach is informal, fresh and pays homage to his New Forest produce and local producers.

Relish Restaurant Rewards
See page 003 for details.

Since opening in 2009 Lime Wood has maintained exceptionally high standards, resulting in being awarded The Sunday Times Travel Editor's Award for excellence in all aspects. Hartnett Holder & Co was also voted Best Hotel Restaurant in September 2014 by Mr & Mrs Smith and Condé Nast Johansens.

'For me, creating great dishes is not about complexity, it is about I how perceive the ingredients and treat them appropriately, to get the very best result.' - Luke Holder, co-head chef, Hartnett Holder & Co.

DOUBLE AGNOLOTTI WITH CHICKEN, POLENTA, PEAS & BROAD BEANS

SERVES 6

 *Dolcetto d'Alba Monte (Italy)*

Ingredients

Pasta

200g pasta flour
9 egg yolks
5ml olive oil

Chicken Filling

500g chicken thighs
2 onions (chopped)
200g lardo di colonnata
500ml light chicken stock
sage (bunch of)
100g aged Parmesan
1 egg yolk

Polenta Filling

200g polenta
100g Parmesan (grated)
olive oil (splash of)
butter (knob of)

Broad Beans And Peas

200g broad beans (*blanched*, shelled)
100g peas (frozen)
1 clove garlic (crushed)
parsley (bunch of, chopped)
butter (knob of)
olive oil (splash of)
salt and pepper

Method

For The Pasta Dough

Blend the flour, egg yolks and oil together in a food processor until a dough is formed. Separate into hand-sized portions, wrap in cling film and refrigerate for 1 hour. Using a pasta machine, roll the dough to a 3mm thickness and trim into 30cm x 8cm sheets.

For The Chicken Filling

Sear the chicken thighs on all sides, then remove. In the same pan, cook the onions without colour. Add the stock and sage, return the thighs and braise until the meat falls from the bone. Drain on kitchen paper, then pull the meat from the bones, skin and sinews. Reduce the *liquor* by two thirds. Blend the meat, reduced stock, lardo di colonnata, Parmesan and egg yolk in a food processor until smooth. Season to taste, then spoon into a piping bag while still warm. Leave to chill until ready to use - the filling should be firm enough to pipe in a solid line.

For The Polenta Filling

Heat the polenta, oil and butter together in a pan over a medium heat, stirring until it thickens. Reduce the heat to low, add the cheese and continue to stir every few minutes until the mixture is a thick consistency. Season to taste, spoon into a piping bag and chill until firm enough to pipe in a solid line.

For The Pasta

Pipe straight lines of the polenta lengthways down the pasta sheets, leaving enough pasta on one side to fold over the filling, then fold the pasta over the top, finally pressing firmly to seal. Moisten the seam to help it stick together.

Use a wheeled pasta cutter to cut the filled tubes of pasta, making sure to keep the sealed strip intact. Using the tips of your fingers, pinch the tube of pasta into equal sized portions, sealing between the pockets each time, then cut with the pasta wheel. Separate the sections with the pasta cutter or a sharp knife. Cook in a large pot of salted boiling water for roughly 2 minutes until tender.

Chef's Tip

Ideally you would have a pasta machine, pasta cutter, Robot Coupe and piping bag.

For The Broad Beans And Peas

Blanch the broad beans and peas in boiling water for 1 minute, then plunge into ice water. Add the garlic, butter and oil to a pan to make an *emulsion*, warm the beans, peas and parsley and season to taste.

Finally, toss in the cooked pasta until evenly coated in the *emulsion*.

To Serve

Spoon onto plates and serve immediately.

RICHARD VAUGHAN'S MIDDLE WHITE PORK CHOP

SERVES 2

 Navarro's Gewürz
(Anderson Valley, USA)

Ingredients

2 x 250g pork chops (*French trimmed*)

Borlotti Beans

200g borlotti beans (fresh)
50g pancetta
1 carrot (chopped)
1 celery stick (chopped)
1 onion (chopped)
1 bulb garlic
a little water (to part cover when braising)

Candied Tomatoes

150g mini San Marzano plum tomatoes
1 lemon (zest of)
100g sugar

To Serve

50ml chicken stock
25ml lemon oil
1 clove garlic (crushed)
saffron (pinch of)
1 lemon (juice of)
1 sprig oregano

Method

For The Borlotti Beans

Braise the borlotti beans with the carrot, celery, pancetta, onion, bulb of garlic and a little water, for about 40 minutes until the beans are soft. Allow to cool in the cooking *liquor*.

For The Candied Tomato

Mix the lemon zest with the sugar. *Blanch* the San Marzano tomatoes in boiling water for 15 seconds, then refresh in iced water. Remove the skin and roll the tomatoes in the lemon sugar. Place on a cake rack and put in the oven at 100°C (fan) for 90 minutes.

For The Pork Chop

Preheat the oven to 180°C (fan).

Chargrill the pork chop for 3 minutes on each side. Place in the oven for 8 minutes, then leave to rest for a further 8 minutes.

To Assemble

Heat the cooked beans with the chicken stock, lemon oil, garlic and saffron. Once hot, add the candied tomatoes, oregano and juice from the lemon. Serve as pictured.

STRAWBERRY CREAM PUFF

SERVES 4 (Each cream puff is a sharing plate for 2 people)

 *Vidal Icewine from Peller Estate
(Ontario, Canada)*

Ingredients

Pastry Cases

1 pack ready-rolled, all butter puff pastry
1 egg (beaten, to wash)
sugar (for sprinkling)

White Chocolate Mousse

375g white chocolate
150ml double cream
1½ leaves gelatine (softened)
500ml whipping cream
2 egg whites

Caramelised White Chocolate Powder

100g white chocolate

To Serve

250g strawberries (trimmed, sliced)
2 sprigs Greek basil

Method

For The Pastry Cases

Lay the pastry flat and cut into 20cm x 12cm rectangles, then carefully score a rectangle 3cm from the edge. Place on a baking tray lined with greaseproof paper, lightly brush with egg wash and sprinkle with sugar. Bake until puffy and golden as per the instructions. Remove from the oven and, very carefully, run a sharp knife around the scoring and lift off the 'lid'.

For The White Chocolate Mousse (Prepare the day before)

Bring the double cream to the boil over a *bain-marie* and separately melt the chocolate over another *bain-marie*.
In 2 separate bowls, whisk the whipping cream and the egg whites to soft peaks.

Dissolve the softened gelatine in the hot cream. Next, *emulsify* the chocolate into the cream by very slowly pouring in the chocolate and continuing to whisk. Fold in the whipped cream, then fold in the whisked egg whites. Spoon some of the mousse into the pastry cases. Place the pastry cases and the remaining mousse into the fridge overnight until set.

For The Caramelised White Chocolate Powder

Preheat the oven to 160°C.

Place the chocolate in the oven on a silpat mat for 20 minutes. The chocolate should melt and caramelise but not fall apart. Finally, remove from the oven, allow to cool, then chop into powdery crumbs.

To Serve

When ready to serve, fill the baskets with strawberries, top with *quenelles* of mousse, sprinkle with caramelised chocolate and garnish with a couple of Greek basil sprigs.

> **Chef's Tip**
> Make sure you have greaseproof paper, a silpat mat and a *bain-marie*.

050
THE TERRACE
AT THE MONTAGU ARMS HOTEL

The Montagu Arms Hotel, Palace Lane, Beaulieu, New Forest, SO42 7ZL

01590 612 324
www.montaguarmshotel.co.uk Twitter: @themontaguarms

Time stands still at the elegant and refined Montagu Arms, which sits on the edge of the New Forest - so close, in fact, that ponies occasionally walk right up to the door.

The Michelin starred restaurant has thrived under the tutelage of classy gastronome Matthew Tomkinson, a Roux scholar, whose precision and artistry dazzles guests in an oak panelled dining room.

Tomkinson is a dizzyingly impressive stylist, whose artful creations are as pretty as a picture. He brings together the best of local, seasonal produce by combining classic combinations and complementary textures.

He is supported by an impressive team: restaurant manager Pierre Rizet Mosser, who formerly worked with top French chef Marc Meneau before a stint at the Roux brothers' Waterside Inn, while head sommelier David Kubler, relocated to the Montagu following stints at Heston Blumenthal's Fat Duck and The Mandarin Grill and Bar, as well as other two star venues.

Tomkinson draws the team together. He achieved his star in 2009 and has retained it since, earning the Montagu a reputation on the national stage, being placed in the top 100 restaurants in the UK by The Times. His kitchen is serviced by an immaculate garden in the hotel's grounds, while close links with an impressive cast of producers help ensure the freshest, best quality ingredients reach guests.

"We are surrounded by land, river and sea, so we have the very best of all worlds. That means we have the pick of nature's larder and we bring it to the plate," says Tomkinson.

Relish Restaurant Rewards
See page 003 for details.

Following the seasons with unfussy, unpretentious and flavoursome food encourages guests to return time and time and time again.

DIVER CAUGHT SCALLOPS WITH CAULIFLOWER PUREE, APPLE, CORIANDER & CUMIN VELOUTE

SERVES 4

 Riesling, Grand Cru, Altenberg De Bergbieten,
Cuvée Henriette, Domaine Frederic Mochel, 2012
(Alsace, France)

Ingredients

Scallops

12 diver caught scallops (opened, cleaned)
2 tbsp ras el hanout

Cumin Velouté

½ small onion (finely sliced)
2 tbsp white wine
4 tbsp cumin seeds (toasted, lightly crushed)
100ml skimmed milk

Cauliflower Purée

1 small cauliflower (cut into florets)
50ml cream (warmed)

Apple And Coriander Salad

½ Granny Smith apple (cut into batons)
½ head fennel (thinly sliced)
20g coriander cress
20g pea shoots

To Finish The Scallops And Salad

1 lemon (juice of)
olive oil
salt (pinch of)
sugar (pinch of)

Method

For The Cumin Velouté

Sweat the onion in a little olive oil until soft, stir in half of the cumin, add the wine and allow to evaporate. Pour in the milk and bring up to 60°C. Add the remaining cumin and pass through a fine sieve. Season and keep warm.

For The Purée

Boil the cauliflower florets in salted water until just tender. Transfer to a blender with the cream and blend to a smooth, light consistency.

For The Scallops

Dip one side of the scallop in the spice and dust off any excess. Fry the scallop in a little olive oil in a hot pan until golden on both sides. Remove and season with salt, a pinch of sugar and a squeeze of juice from the lemon.

> **Chef's Tip**
>
> Try to source diver caught scallops. They really are worth the extra money and are much kinder to the environment.

For The Apple And Coriander Salad

In a small bowl, toss the pea shoots, coriander cress, apple and fennel together. Squeeze in a few drops of lemon juice, a few drops of olive oil and a pinch each of salt and sugar.

To Serve

Place a large spoon of purée and 3 scallops on 4 warmed plates. Divide the apple salad between the plates. Using a hand blender, froth up the sauce and spoon a few of the bubbles over the dish to serve.

ROAST SADDLE OF ORGANIC LAMB WITH BRAISED SHOULDER, CRISPY SWEETBREAD, ANNA POTATO

SERVES 4

 Montsant, La Universal, Venus, Sara Pérez & René Barbier, 2007 (Catalonia, Spain)

Ingredients

4 quality lamb and rosemary sausages
½ short saddle of lamb (cut lengthways, boned, trimmed, seasoned)

Lamb Shoulder

½ shoulder lamb (seasoned)
500ml good lamb stock (hot)
small bunch chives (finely chopped)

Sweetbreads

4 large lamb sweetbreads (soaked for 24 hours in cold water)
1 lemon (squeeze of)
small sprig rosemary
50g panko breadcrumbs
1 egg (beaten)
20g plain flour
salt
sugar (pinch of)

Anna Potatoes

4 large Maris Piper potatoes (peeled, thinly sliced)
200ml duck fat (warmed)
4 cloves garlic (crushed)
sprig rosemary
salt

To Serve

200g rainbow chard or spinach (washed, dried, *sautéed* in olive oil, seasoned with salt)

4 small wooden kebab skewers

Method

For The Lamb Shoulder
Preheat the oven to 120ºC (fan).
Brown the lamb in a little oil in a casserole pot. Pour in the stock, cover and braise for 3 hours until tender.
Leave to cool in the liquid until hand hot. Remove and pick the meat. Pass the liquid through a fine sieve, skim off any fat and reduce to a sauce consistency.

For The Sweetbreads (Allow over 24 hours)
Rinse the soaked sweetbreads and put into fresh, cold water with the rosemary, a squeeze of lemon, salt and sugar. Bring to a simmer, then remove from the heat. Leave to cool completely in the liquid. Once cool, carefully peel away any membrane. Dry well, toss in a little flour, dip in the beaten egg, then roll in the breadcrumbs. Reserve in the fridge.

> **Chef's Tip**
> Many people are put off trying sweetbreads but they have a delicious mild lamb flavour and really are worth including in the dish.

For The Anna Potatoes (Make the day before)
Infuse the duck fat with the rosemary, garlic and salt for 1 hour. Pass through a sieve. Line a small dish with baking parchment. Layer the potato slices, to a minimum of 2.5cm deep, in the dish with a good spoonful of fat and a pinch of salt on each layer. Cover with parchment and then foil. Place in a *bain-marie* in an oven (180ºC) until cooked through (check with knife). Cool for 1 hour. Place a weight on top and refrigerate overnight. Cut 4 nice pieces from it - keep cold.

For The Saddle
Preheat the oven to 200ºC (fan).
Place skin-side down in a hot pan with a little oil and cook until the skin is crispy. Reduce the heat, turn the meat over and colour a little, then turn again. Place in the oven for 5 minutes. Remove the meat from the pan and rest in a warm place.

To Serve
Heat a fryer to 180ºC. Place the potato portions in the oven (200ºC) for 20 minutes and the sausages for 12 minutes. Reheat the shoulder meat in a little reserved lamb sauce. Season and add the chives. Deep fry the sweetbreads until golden, then season. Skewer the sweetbread and sausage on the skewers. Carve the saddle into 4 and divide all elements between 4 hot plates. Serve at once.

DARK CHOCOLATE CREMEUX, WALNUT ICE CREAM, COFFEE MACARON & MILK CHOCOLATE MOUSSE

SERVES 8

 Vigna del Volta, Emilia Malvasia Passito, La Stoppa 2008 (Italy)

Ingredients

Walnut Paste And Ice Cream
300g walnuts
270g sugar
10ml hazelnut oil
480ml full-fat milk
600ml water
120g skimmed milk powder
12g cremidor emulsifier
40g egg yolks (approximately 2 eggs)

Dark Chocolate Crémeux
120g 70% dark chocolate (broken into pieces)
3 egg yolks, 25g caster sugar
130ml full-fat milk, 130ml whipping cream

Coffee Macarons
120g egg whites (3-4 eggs)
8g instant coffee granules
125g ground almonds
125g icing sugar (sifted), 125g caster sugar

Coffee Ganache
100ml whipping cream, 5g ground coffee
100g white chocolate (broken into pieces)

Milk Chocolate Mousse
275ml whipping cream, 50ml milk
30g egg yolks (1-2 eggs), 15g caster sugar
300g 34% milk chocolate (broken into pieces)

Chocolate Soil
50g caster sugar, 50g ground almonds
30g plain flour, 22g cocoa powder
35g unsalted butter (melted), 3g salt
(Combine all the soil ingredients and bake on a non-stick tray at 160°C (fan) for 8 minutes. Cool)

Garnish
candied walnuts, coffee purée, chocolate sauce, chocolate strands

Method

For The Walnut Paste And Ice Cream (Allow 8 hours)
Roast the walnuts in the hazelnut oil for 8 minutes at 200°C. Cook the nuts with 150g sugar to a caramel. Cool, then blend to a paste.

Combine the water, milk powder and milk and bring to 40°C over a medium heat. Stir in 60g sugar and the cremidor until dissolved. Whisk 60g sugar with the egg yolks until pale, then add to the warm milk. Stirring continuously, bring to 85°C. When it reaches temperature, pour onto 200g of the walnut paste, combine well and chill for 6 hours. Pass through a fine sieve and churn in an ice cream machine.

For The Dark Chocolate Crémeux
Boil the milk and whipping cream. Whisk the egg yolks and sugar until pale and pour the hot cream onto the egg mixture, whisking constantly. Place back into the pan and cook until thickened and will coat the back of a spoon. Pass through a fine sieve onto the chocolate and mix well. Place in a plastic container in the fridge to set for 2 hours.

For The Coffee Macarons
Place half the egg whites in a mixing bowl with the coffee and mix well. Leave for 15 minutes to allow the coffee to dissolve. Add the icing sugar and ground almonds and beat to a thick paste. Place the remaining egg whites and caster sugar into a mixing bowl and whisk gently to dissolve the sugar. Place the bowl over a *bain-marie* and, using an electric whisk, beat until 65°C. Remove from the heat, continue whisking until it cools and forms stiff peaks. Gently fold this Swiss meringue into the coffee paste until smooth. Pipe circles (size of a £1 coin) onto a non-stick mat. Leave to dry for 25 minutes. Cook at 150°C for 12 minutes, reduce the temperature to 140°C and cook for a further 5 minutes. Allow to cool.

For The Coffee Ganache
Boil the cream, add the coffee and pass through a fine sieve onto the chocolate. Mix well and place in the fridge to set.

For The Milk Chocolate Mousse
Boil the milk and 50ml of cream. Whisk the eggs and sugar until pale, then pour the hot cream onto the egg mixture whisking constantly. Place back into the pan and cook until 84°C. Pass through a fine sieve onto the chocolate and mix well. Place over a *bain-marie* to make sure the chocolate is completely melted. Allow to cool to room temperature and fold in the remaining cream that has been whipped to soft peaks. Place in the fridge to set.

To Serve
Sandwich the macarons together using the coffee ganache. Garnish with chocolate soil and be creative!

060
THE WHITE HORSE HOTEL & BRASSERIE

19 Market Place, Romsey, Hampshire, SO51 8ZJ

01794 512 431
www.thewhitehorseromsey.co.uk Twitter: @WHRomsey Facebook: TheWhiteHorseHotelandBrasserie

Modern British classics and buttery, hand-selected steaks, provide food for thought at The White Horse Hotel and Brasserie, in Romsey.

The Grade II listed hotel is one of only three late-medieval structures in Hampshire that were devised as purpose-built inns. Since its inception in the late 15th Century, it has been remodelled and re-imagined, while remaining true to the original.

The White Horse provides guests with a luxurious environment in which to relax, with its lofty penthouse suite popular with guests and newlyweds alike.

An accessible menu provides the best of British, while diners can also eat the region's finest steaks, courtesy of the Big Bertha charcoal grill. Head chef Nick O'Halloran cooks the finest 35 day aged, corn fed American and British steaks to his customers' specifications.

The venue has a firm and binding commitment to the best of local produce. It is a member of the Hampshire Fare Group and is committed to sourcing local produce from within a 30 mile radius wherever possible.

The White Horse offers sublime afternoon teas and extravagant breakfasts, as well as an impressive à la carte menu each evening. There are cases and cases of unusual teas from which to choose, not to mention an extraordinary 100 bottle whisky cellar, which features some of the most exclusive and hard to find bottles in the world.

Relish Restaurant Rewards
See page 003 for details.

The 21st Century incarnation mixes trend and tradition, with original features alongside stylish, contemporary fittings.

NEW FOREST WILD MUSHROOM RAGU, LEEK, CONFIT TOMATO & GARLIC, FRIED QUAIL EGG

SERVES 4

 Kim Crawford Pinot Noir, Marlborough (New Zealand)

Ingredients

Wild Mushroom Ragu

250g mixed wild mushrooms
(washed of any dirt or grit)
1 banana shallot (thinly sliced)
1 clove garlic (crushed)
1 sprig thyme
15g marmite
15g tomato purée
10ml white wine
25ml water
1 tsp oil

Garlic And Tomato Confit

1 punnet cherry tomatoes
1 bulb garlic (peeled)
rapeseed oil (to cover)
2 sprigs thyme
sea salt (pinch of)

To Serve

1 large leek (split lengthways, washed)
parsley purée
4 quail eggs

Method

For The Wild Mushroom Ragu

Sauté the mushrooms in a hot pan with the oil until they begin to colour. Add a pinch of salt followed by the shallots, garlic and thyme and cook until soft. Add the tomato purée and marmite, cook out slightly, then add the wine and water and allow to reduce to a thick sauce consistency. Adjust seasoning.

> **Chef's Tip**
>
> Try to source the best mushrooms available in season.
> If foraging for your own, please research what you have picked as some can be poisonous.

For The Garlic Confit

Reserve 1 garlic clove and submerge the rest of the garlic in the rapeseed oil. Cook at a very low heat for about 45 minutes until soft and sweet.

For The Tomato Confit

Preheat the oven to 80°C.

Chop the remaining garlic clove and add the thyme with a pinch of sea salt. Cut the tomatoes in half and toss in 1 tablespoon of oil with the chopped garlic and thyme mix. Place on a wire rack and cook for about 1 hour.

To Serve

Cut the leek into approximately 5cm lengths and *blanch* in seasoned water for 90 seconds, drain onto a j-cloth, brush with melted butter and season.

Fry the quail eggs and season with sea salt.

Place some parsley purée on the plate. Add a spoon of the ragu, the same length as the leek, then top with a slice of leek. Repeat this process once more and finish with a spoon of the mushroom ragu. Top with the quail egg and scatter the tomatoes and *confit* garlic around the plate with a drizzle of extra virgin rapeseed oil.

WEST WELLOW PORK, CARROT PUREE, BLACK PUDDING POTATO CAKE, CIDER SAUCE

SERVES 4

 Camille Cayran 'Impatiente'
(Southern Rhône, France)

Ingredients

1 x 500g pork fillet
500g pork belly

Pig Cheeks

4 pig cheeks
1 carrot (chopped)
1 onion (chopped)
1 stick celery (chopped)
red wine (to *deglaze*)

Potato Cake

1 large baking potato
75g quality black pudding
flour
egg
panko breadcrumbs

Carrot Purée

4 large carrots (peeled, sliced)
100g butter

Cider Sauce

100ml chicken stock
100ml cider

To Serve

100g spinach
butter (knob of)

Method

Chef's Tip

It's best to prepare the pork belly and pig cheek a day in advance to get best results. It will then give you some time to get the sauce just right!

For The Pork Belly

Preheat the oven to 200°C.

Season the belly and place in a deep roasting tray. Fill with water half way up the belly, oil the skin and salt generously. Roast for 20 minutes. Lower the oven to 150°C, cover with foil and cook for a further 3-3½ hours. Remove the belly and press between 2 trays. Retain the cooking *liquor* for the sauce.

For The Pig Cheeks

Preheat the oven to 150°C.

Season the cheeks and seal in a hot frying pan. Add the *mirepoix* of vegetables and *deglaze* with red wine. Transfer to a deep tray, cover with cold water and cook in the oven for 2-3 hours.

For The Potato Cake

Preheat the oven to 200°C.

Bake the potato until soft, scoop out the flesh from its skin and pass through a potato ricer. Add the black pudding and season well. Weigh into 50g balls and shape in a ring. *Panne* the cakes using the flour, egg and panko breadcrumbs.

For The Carrot Purée

Cover the carrots with water, bring to the boil and cook until soft. Strain and place into a food processor with the butter and purée until smooth. Pass through a fine sieve and season.

For The Sauce

Add the cider, the pork cooking juices and the chicken stock to a saucepan and reduce to a sauce consistency.

To Serve

Portion the pork belly, season the pork fillet and seal in a pan on all sides. Cook in a preheated oven at 180°C for 6-7 minutes, then rest. Put the cheeks in the cider sauce.

Deep fry (190°C) the potato cake for 2-3 minutes until golden. *Sauté* the spinach in butter.

Trim the fillet and cut into 4 portions. Assemble the plate as pictured.

STICKY TOFFEE FONDANT, VANILLA ICE CREAM, DATES

SERVES 8

 Bristol Cream Sweet Sherry

Ingredients

Date Purée

250g pitted dates
300ml water
15g bicarbonate of soda

Salted Caramel

125g soft brown sugar
100ml double cream
sea salt (pinch of)

Sponge

5 eggs
175g caster sugar
175g butter (melted)
200g date purée (see above)
300g plain flour

Vanilla Ice Cream

250ml full-fat milk
150ml double cream
50g egg yolk (2-3 eggs)
75g caster sugar
1 vanilla pod

To Serve

chocolate soil
pistachio nuts (chopped)

8 *dariole* moulds (6½cm x 6cm)

Method

For The Date Purée

Bring the dates and water to the boil, add the bicarbonate of soda and blitz in liquidiser. Cool immediately.

For The Salted Caramel

Bring the ingredients to a simmer, then gently boil for approximately 4 minutes. Set in the fridge.

To Make The Sponge

Whisk the eggs and sugar until *sabayon*. Mix together the melted butter and 200g of the date purée. Whisk into the egg *sabayon* and fold in the flour.

For The Vanilla Ice Cream

Bring the milk, cream and vanilla pod to the boil. Whisk the eggs and sugar until pale, then pour over the hot vanilla milk whilst mixing.

Pour back into pan and, over a medium heat, cook out the eggs, stirring continuously, until it resembles a thick custard.

Pass through a sieve. When cool, churn in an ice cream machine.

To Assemble And Serve

Preheat the oven to 180°C.

Butter and sugar the *dariole* moulds. Place 80g of the sponge mixture into each mould.

Ball 25g of the salted caramel and push into the sponge mixture, closing the gap it went through.

Rest the mixture.

Bake for 10 minutes, remove from the oven and allow to rest for 2 minutes.

Spread some of the date purée on the plate, sprinkle with the chopped pistachios and chocolate soil. Ball the ice cream and place at one end, next to the fondant.

Chef's Tip

Have the mix in the moulds well in advance of when needed. The 2 minutes resting after cooking are just as important as the cooking time.

SUSSEX, LAND OF PLENTY

Introduction by Matt Gillan, Head Chef, Matt Gillan at The Pass

I have been fortunate enough to have worked in some of the best restaurants in the country and have been exposed to the best produce available during the process. These former years have set the precedent to what I deem acceptable to serve in my restaurant.

Without the quality to begin with, you can't produce a satisfactory end result. We are fortunate enough in Sussex to have the best produce available to us on our doorstep. And the range is vast. From tomatoes in Nutbourne, to game in Petworth. Fish from the day boats, to Japanese leaves and vegetables in Lewes. Not to mention quails, the first Sussex wagyu cross beef, asparagus, mushrooms, an amazing range of cheese, award-winning breweries and the best sparkling wines in the country.

Sussex has given us chefs a variety of produce, allowing us to be creative with our offerings whilst retaining our individuality. This is reflected in the diverse range of country house hotels, restaurants and pubs. From Michelin stars to beach-side cafés, there is something for everyone's taste, and all delivered to a high standard.

I've spent the last nine years in Sussex and love finding new, small producers offering amazing ingredients and new eateries tucked away in the nooks and crannies, all showcasing the quality this region has to offer.

AMBERLEY CASTLE

Amberley, Arundel, West Sussex, BN18 9LT

01798 831 992
www.amberleycastle.co.uk Twitter: @amberleycastle Facebook: Amberley Castle

L ocated in a picturesque village on the doorstep of the South Downs National Park, Amberley Castle is a unique, luxury hotel steeped in over 900 years of history. Within the medieval walls of this enchanting retreat, executive chef Robby Jenks has created a delicious and original menu using the best of British and local produce, cooked to perfection and complemented by modern European influences.

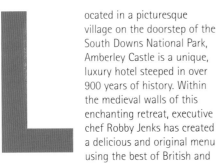

Having started his career at sister property Gidleigh Park, Robby has spent years honing his craft and skills before taking the reins at Amberley Castle almost two years ago. Robby's ethos is simple and contemporary, focusing on an unfussy, elegant dining experience in which exceptional ingredients are cooked to the highest standards. This inspirational style of cuisine, blended with the talent and passion of Robby and his team, has been the driving force in achieving three AA Rosettes.

Relish Restaurant Rewards
See page 003 for details.

Guests are invited to step back in time at Amberley Castle; suits of armour stand to attention, intricate coats of arms tell tales of previous owners and fine fabrics sit alongside beautiful antiques.

LOBSTER WITH BLACK CURRY MAYONNAISE, WATERMELON & RADISH

SERVES 4

 Domaine Christian Binner, "Les Saveurs...", 2013, Alsace (France)
A blend of Chasselas, Muscat, Pinot Blanc Sylvaner.
Wine recommendations courtesy of Pawel Nowinski.

Ingredients

1 lobster (whole)

Black Curry Mayonnaise

10g black curry powder (any curry powder will work depending on how hot you like it)
10ml vegetable oil
150g mayonnaise
150g Greek yoghurt
salt
1 lime (juice of)

To Serve

Greek yoghurt (to bind)
basil leaves (chopped)
1 lime (shavings and juice of)
100g watermelon (diced)
5 radishes (sliced)
basil and sorrel leaves (optional)
citrus jelly cubes (optional)

Method

For The Lobster

Prepare the lobster - tie a spoon along its tail to keep it straight and ensure an accurate cooking time. Cook the tail for 3-4 minutes and leave to rest for 5 minutes before placing in ice water. The claws should be cooked for 5-6 minutes, depending on size, then placed in ice water. They are cooked when the claw releases cleanly from the bone. Once cool, peel the lobster pieces and set aside. Cut the tail into pieces, saving the claw meat for later.

Chef's Tip

Freeze live lobsters for 2 hours to slow their metabolism before preparation. Prepare the lobster by resting a knife blade along the length of its head and pressing down with force, swiftly. Separate the claws and tail, discarding the body and head.

For The Black Curry Mayonnaise

Lightly toast the curry powder in a small pan, then add the vegetable oil and leave to infuse whilst preparing the rest of the dish. After the oil has infused, mix the mayonnaise and Greek yoghurt together before adding to the infusion. Season the mix with salt and lime juice to taste.

To Serve

Finely dice the claw meat and bind with Greek yoghurt, adding chopped basil and lime juice to taste. Place the chopped lobster tail on the plate with the watermelon and radishes, then dress with the claw meat mix and mayonnaise. Garnish with lime shavings, basil and sorrel leaves.

For special occasions, bring some extra colour to your plate by decorating with citrus jelly cubes.

BEST END LAMB WITH CONFIT TOMATO, AUBERGINE & FONDANT POTATO

SERVES 4

 Jochen Dreissigacker, 'Wunderwerk', 2011, Wonnegau, Germany (Pinot Noir)

Ingredients

Lamb

best end lamb (ask your butcher for a best end cut, although any will do)
butter (knob of)
250g dried breadcrumbs
125g fresh parsley
50ml olive oil, 2 cloves garlic

Lamb Sauce

1kg lamb carcasses (chopped into small pieces)
50ml olive oil (plus extra for frying)
50g each onions, leeks, carrots (chopped into small pieces)
½ bulb garlic
200g ripe plum tomatoes
50g tomato purée
5g each fresh thyme and rosemary
1g each cumin seeds and cinnamon
100ml water
750ml chicken stock
200ml beef stock

Confit Tomatoes

16 cherry tomatoes
olive oil (to drizzle)
salt and pepper (to season)

Aubergine

1 aubergine (sliced)
30ml balsamic vinegar
130ml olive oil (plus extra for frying)
4 basil leaves

Fondant Potato

4 baking potatoes (peeled)
125g unsalted butter
1 sprig thyme, 1 bay leaf
2 garlic cloves

Garnish

seasonal vegetables (optional)

Method

For The Lamb

Prepare the lamb as per your butcher's instructions for the cut, then brown in a pan with a knob of butter. Place in an oven at 160°C until cooked to your liking. Remove the lamb from the oven and rest for 10 minutes.

Blend the breadcrumbs to a fine crumb. Add in the parsley and garlic, slowly pouring in the olive oil as it blends. Season the crumb mix to taste and press firmly onto the rested lamb.

For The Lamb Sauce

Roast the lamb carcasses in the oven at 200°C until golden brown, about 1 hour.

In a separate pan, sweat the onions, leeks, garlic bulb and carrots in 50ml olive oil. Add the thyme, rosemary, cumin seeds and cinnamon and sweat for a further 5 minutes, then add the tomatoes and tomato purée, cooking out for 10 minutes.

Once roasted, place the lamb carcasses into the vegetable compôte, adding the water, beef stock and chicken stock. Bring to the boil, reducing the temperature to simmer for 30 minutes. Pass the mixture through a colander and fine sieve to reduce the consistency before passing through a muslin cloth.

For The Confit Tomatoes

Slice the tomatoes in half and place on a tray with a little olive oil, seasoning lightly and bake at 70°C for 3 hours.

For The Aubergine Purée (Best prepared the day before)

Heat a little oil in a pan and place the aubergine in, seasoning to taste and turning until cooked. Place it in a marinade mixture of the basil, vinegar and 100ml olive oil, leaving for at least 2 hours in the fridge.

To prepare the aubergine purée, wrap the marinated aubergine in tin foil with 30ml of olive oil and bake at 180°C for 1 hour until soft. Blend and reserve for later.

> **Chef's Tip**
> Prepare your aubergine the day before and allow it to marinate longer.

For The Fondant Potato

Using a cutter, trim the potatoes to approximately 5cm in diameter. Melt the butter in a pan with the thyme, bay leaf and garlic cloves, placing the potatoes in once hot. Allow the butter to melt around the potatoes, colouring lightly and cooking until tender. Allow to cool in the butter.

To Serve

Set your prepared lamb on the plate and dress with the lamb sauce, tomatoes, aubergine purée and fondant potato, serving with a seasonal vegetable accompaniment of your choice. Stuffed bell peppers and oven-roast baby onions work particularly well.

LYCHEE MACARON

SERVES 4

🍷 *Franz Haas, Moscato Rosa, "Schweizer", 2011,*
Trentino Alto Adige (Italy)

Ingredients

Lychee Sorbet

500g lychee purée
150ml stock syrup (boiling water and sugar)
1 lemon (juice of)

Macaron

300g icing sugar
180g ground almonds
150g egg whites
35g caster sugar
red food colouring (dash of)

Raspberry Jelly

100g raspberry purée
5ml Eau de Vie Mirabelle
25ml water
2g gelatine (soaked)
1g sea salt

Rose Ganache

65ml whipping cream
4ml rose water
100g white chocolate (broken up)

Garnish

fresh raspberries

Method

For The Lychee Sorbet (Prepare ahead)
Blend the lychee purée, stock syrup and lemon juice together and freeze.

For The Macaron
Sift the icing sugar and ground almonds together. Beat 75g egg whites until firm, adding the caster sugar and pouring on the remaining egg whites, then beat once again. Fold in the icing sugar and ground almonds gently until smooth, adding a dash of food colouring. Do not over mix. Pipe into discs, approximately 5cm across, and cook at 160ºC for approximately 10 minutes.

> **Chef's Tip**
>
> For larger quantities, cook all of the macarons at the same time to ensure consistent cooking. Every macaron is different however, so keep a close eye as they cook.

For The Raspberry Jelly
Soak the gelatine in cold water to soften. Combine the 25ml of water with the alcohol and bring to the boil. Stir in the gelatine until dissolved. Mix in the salt and raspberry purée before setting on a tray to cut out later. Set in the fridge for 3-4 hours.

For The Rose Ganache
Combine the whipping cream and rose water in a small pan, bringing it to the boil. Remove from the heat before adding the chocolate. Beat together until the chocolate has melted into the cream. Allow to cool.

To Serve
Place a disc of the jelly on a plate, with the macaron and ganache on top. Arrange a handful of fresh raspberries on the ganache and top with a scoop of lychee sorbet.

082
THE CHEQUERS INN

Rohook, Nr Horsham, West Sussex, RH12 3PY

01403 790 480
www.thechequersrowhook.com

Husband and wife team Tim and Katy Neal conjured a must-visit dining destination almost from thin air when they created The Chequers Inn, at Rowhook.

The couple purchased the run-down, near-derelict former pub just after the Millennium. Their hard work transformed the venue into a popular and sought after destination among the south east's discerning diners. There are Horsham flagstones, oak beams, stripped floorboards and roaring log fires.

Chequers Inn features in the Michelin, Hardens and AA guides. It is a cut above other gastropubs along the Surrey and Sussex border.

Housed in a lovely old 15th Century cottage that is tucked away, well off the beaten track, it is in one of the region's most peaceful and bucolic locations.

Chef-patron Tim is a Master Chef of Great Britain and offers unpretentious food that bursts with flavour. He works alongside head chef Craig Goldsmith to create well-cooked dishes that feature the best of seasonal ingredients.

Tim says, "We have a larder right here on our doorstep. We can literally step outside the door and find truffles, farmers producing great meat or sensational fruit and vegetables."

The reputation of Chequers Inn means it has a starry clientele with many A-listers regularly popping in. Not that Tim and Katy forget their locals. They maintain a bar for regulars and serve the best local ales from the south east.

Katy adds, "It's all about creating great flavours and a brilliant atmosphere in which people can relax."

The promise of cleverly-constructed dishes, perfect flavour pairings and hospitable service makes Chequers a class apart.

Relish Restaurant Rewards
See page 003 for details.

At The Chequers Inn, the food is unpretentious. The best ingredients, cooked well.

Over the past 13 years Tim and his team have forged a reputation for providing one of the best dining experiences in the south.

BACON ROLY POLY, BEER MUSTARD MAYONNAISE, FRIED QUAIL EGG

SERVES 4

 Villa Wolf Pinot Gris
(Pfalz, Germany)

Ingredients

4 fresh quail eggs

Bacon Roly Poly

365g plain flour
180g suet
baking powder (pinch of)
salt (pinch of)
6 rashers dry cured bacon
210ml cold water

Beer Mustard Mayonnaise

4 egg yolks
2 dsp Tracklements beer mustard
1 dsp white wine vinegar
1 dsp cold water
350ml vegetable oil
salt and white pepper (to season)

Garnish

salad leaves

Method

For The Bacon Roly Poly

Place the dry ingredients in a bowl, add the cold water and work together until a dough consistency.

Roll the dough out on a floured table into a 24cm square. Place the bacon over the suet pastry, roll it up into a sausage shape using cling film and tie at both ends.

Place the roly poly into a pan of simmering water and cook for 40 minutes. Remove the pan from the heat and allow the roly poly to cool in the water.

Once cooled, remove the cling film and cut into 2cm discs, allowing 3 per person. Heat a frying pan on a medium heat, add a little oil and fry the roly poly on both sides until brown.

For The Beer Mustard Mayonnaise

Combine the egg yolks, mustard, vinegar and water in a bowl. Add the oil in a small trickle and whisk very slowly until it is completely incorporated.

Add salt and pepper to taste.

To Fry The Quail Eggs

Crack the eggs into a warm pan with a little oil and fry until cooked.

> **Chef's Tip**
>
> Keep the quail egg yolks soft as this adds another sauce to the dish.

To Serve

Arrange the roly poly, mayonnaise and fried quail egg on a plate. Garnish with salad leaves.

PAN FRIED SUSSEX LOIN OF VENISON, PARSNIP & VANILLA PUREE, SAUTEED AUTUMN CHANTERELLES, BUTTERED SAVOY CABBAGE & PORT WINE SAUCE

SERVES 4

 Felino Malbec Viña Cobos Mendoza
(Argentina)

Ingredients

4 x 250g pieces venison

Parsnip And Vanilla Purée

2 medium parsnips (peeled, medium diced)
300ml water
100g unsalted butter
⅓ vanilla pod (scraped)
150ml double cream
salt and ground white pepper

Port Wine Sauce

6 shallots (diced)
1 carrot (diced)
1 stick celery (diced)
1 bay leaf
1 sprig thyme
568ml venison or beef stock
250ml port
150ml red wine
50ml cassis

Buttered Savoy Cabbage

600g Savoy cabbage (thinly shredded)
butter (knob of)

Autumn Chanterelles

100g chanterelles
butter (knob of)

Parsnip Crisps

1 parsnip (peeled)

Method

For The Parsnip And Vanilla Purée

Place the parsnips into a saucepan with the water, butter and vanilla. Cook over a medium heat, allowing the liquid to evaporate, until the parsnips are soft. Add the cream, cook for another 5 minutes, then blend in a food processor. Remove and season to taste.

To Make The Port Wine Sauce

Add the vegetables to a hot pan with a little oil and caramelise until brown. Add the bay leaf, thyme, stock, port, red wine and cassis. Reduce by a third and season. Pass through a fine sieve.

For The Buttered Savoy Cabbage

Place the shredded cabbage into salted, boiling water and cook for 3 minutes. Remove from the heat and strain. Place into a bowl, add a knob of butter, then season.

For The Venison

Preheat the oven to 180°C.
Season the venison with salt and pepper, then place into a hot, ovenproof frying pan with a little oil and butter. Cook the venison on both sides until golden brown, approximately 2 minutes each side.
Transfer to the oven for 8 minutes. Remove and leave to rest for 2 minutes to allow the meat to relax.

> **Chef's Tip**
> Once cooked, wrap the venison in cling film to retain the cooking juices. These can be added to the sauce.

For The Autumn Chanterelles

Wash the mushrooms in cold water and pat dry in a clean cloth. *Sauté* in a little butter and season.

For The Parsnip Crisps

Using a potato peeler, peel fine strips from the parsnip and deep fry until golden brown. Remove and place on some kitchen towel to remove any excess oil.

To Serve

Warm the cabbage and place in a ring. Slice the venison and arrange on top. Sprinkle the wild mushrooms, dot the purée and port wine sauce onto the plate. Garnish with deep fried parsnip crisps.

ORANGE & CARDAMOM PANNA COTTA WITH HONEY ROASTED FIGS

SERVES 4

 Brigaldara Recioto della Valpolicella (Italy)

Ingredients

Orange And Cardamom Panna Cotta

568ml double cream
1 orange (zest of)
½ orange (juice of)
4 cardamom pods (crushed)
65g caster sugar
2½ leaves gelatine (softened in cold water)

Honey Roasted Figs

4 fresh figs (cut in half)
25g unsalted butter
50g runny honey
½ vanilla pod (scraped)

4 x 200ml *dariole* moulds

Method

For Orange And Cardamom Panna Cotta (Best made the day before)

Place the double cream, orange zest, orange juice, cardamom pods and caster sugar in a saucepan. Bring to the boil, then remove from the heat.

Squeeze the gelatine leaves to remove the water and add to the cream mixture, stirring until the gelatine has dissolved. Pass through a fine sieve, pour into the moulds and place in the fridge until set, approximately 2 hours.

For The Honey Roasted Figs

Place the cut figs into a hot pan with the butter, vanilla and honey. Cook over a medium heat until soft, approximately 5 minutes. Remove from the heat and leave to cool in the pan.

To Serve

Run the panna cotta moulds under a warm tap to loosen them. Turn out onto plates, place the figs around and drizzle the fig cooking juices over the panna cotta.

092
DEANS PLACE HOTEL

Seaford Road, Alfriston, East Sussex, BN26 5TW

01323 870 248
www.deansplacehotel.co.uk Twitter: @DeansPlaceHotel

Sophisticated food amid sumptuous surroundings make Deans Place Hotel a home from home. The family run country hotel and restaurant is set in splendid East Sussex countryside, providing a welcome retreat at a gentle pace of life.

The ownership of Michael Clinch and management of his son-in-law and daughter, James and Lucinda Dopson, ushered in a new era for the quintessentially English period property, which sits amongst splendid gardens, immaculately maintained lawns and has an idyllic view across the Cuckmere River.

Head chef Stuart Dunley's eight year tenure has also seen the restaurant grow in popularity within the region and has been awarded 2 AA Rosettes since 2010. His modern British cuisine, inspired by the best of local, seasonal produce and his exceptional connections with independent artisans ensures the best ingredients for diners.

"Being surrounded by farms and so close to the sea, we have a rich array of local produce, which is a joy to work with and helps make our food so appealing to our diners," he says.

Guests can also ease away their troubles in comfortable and relaxing rooms, which mix trend and tradition. Heavy beams hark back to a bygone era, while new mod cons mean visitors are left wanting for nothing. With an all-day food offering, Deans Place is available from breakfast through lunch, afternoon tea and into dinner.

"We are set in one of the most beautiful locations in the UK," says James Dopson. "Great food, exceptional service and a stunning location encourage our guests to return time and time again."

 Relish Restaurant Rewards
See page 003 for details.

Guests can relax and enjoy a tranquil environment where time seems to stand still, although constant reinvestment means Deans Place is forever moving forward and an impressively refurbished restaurant is its latest attraction.

FISH PIE FONDANT

SERVES 6

 Puligny-Montrachet, Louis Latour (France)

Ingredients

6 x 600-800g sea bass fillets (scaled, pin boned - ask your fishmonger to scale and remove the bones from the fillets)

Mashed Potato
180g potato (peeled)
saffron (pinch of)
salt (pinch of)
1 egg yolk
25g Parmesan (freshly grated)
30g butter (melted)

Pea Purée
120g peas (shelled)
150ml milk
salt (pinch of)
nutmeg (pinch of)

Scallop Mousse
200g scallop meat (no roe)
150ml double cream
3g salt
1 egg white

To Serve
seasonal fish of your choice (here we used razor clams, scallops and salmon)

Garnish
fresh tomato (diced)
pea shoots

6cm x 4cm deep x 6-7cm diameter metal, or ovenproof ring moulds
piping bag and a star nozzle
greaseproof or silicone paper

Method

For The Mashed Potato
Add the saffron to a pan of boiling water and simmer the potatoes until tender. Pass the hot potatoes through a sieve or potato ricer to remove any lumps. Stir through the egg yolk, Parmesan and butter, then spoon into a piping bag.

For The Pea Purée
Place the peas in the milk with the seasoning, bring to the boil and simmer for 2 minutes. Reserve 20g of the peas. Blend the remainder to a purée, stir through the reserved peas and chill in the fridge.

For The Scallop Mousse
Blend the scallops with the egg white, salt and double cream in a food processor. Do not over blend or the mousse will curdle. Chill in the fridge.

To Assemble The Dish
Line the moulds on the inside with baking parchment, then butter this to prevent the fish from sticking. Line the fish around the inside, with the skin to the outside.

Apply a layer of the mousse against the white flesh of the sea bass all the way around and on the base, retaining some of the mousse to go on the top once the pea purée is added.

Add 2 dessertspoons of the pea purée, cover with the remaining scallop mousse and chill for 20 minutes.

Pipe the potato onto the top, lightly butter the potato and add a sprinkling of Parmesan.

To Serve
Preheat the oven to 190°C (fan).

Bake the fondant on a tray lined with parchment to protect the base, for 13 minutes. Remove from the oven and allow to set back for 5 minutes in a warm place, otherwise the fondant will be too hot and delicate to remove from the mould. Arrange on a plate using a fish slice. Serve with your favourite, in season fish, or on its own.

Chef's Tip
Allow the cooked fondant to set back otherwise it could collapse when trying to remove it from the ring mould. Ensure all ingredients are chilled before assembling the pie.

SPICED VENISON, SALT BAKED CELERIAC, HONEY SOUSED BEETROOT

SERVES 4

 *Brown Brothers Limited Release Shiraz
(Australia)*

Ingredients

Spiced Venison

1 long venison loin
1 tbsp juniper berries
3 tbsp pink peppercorns
3 tbsp panko breadcrumbs
2 tbsp rapeseed oil
1 tbsp sea salt
2 tbsp honey

Salt Baked Celeriac

1 celeriac (trimmed)
550g plain flour
650g salt
8 large, free range egg whites
150ml double cream
50g unsalted butter
salt and pepper

Honey Soused Beetroot

a good selection of beetroots (eg golden, candy,
baby, purple)
1 banana shallot (finely sliced)
100ml groundnut oil
50ml hazelnut oil
2 sprigs thyme
1 tbsp dry sherry
1 tbsp Merlot vinegar
1 lime (zest and juice of)

Jus

500g venison bones
2 litres good game stock (or chicken stock)
250ml port, 250ml Madeira
1 onion, 1 carrot
2 sticks celery
1 leek
1 bulb garlic
4 juniper berries, 8 peppercorns
1 bay leaf, 1 sprig thyme
1 bunch black grapes

Method

For The Salt Baked Celeriac

Preheat the oven to 155°C (fan).

Mix the flour, salt, egg whites and water in a bowl. Cover the trimmed celeriac in paste so there are no gaps and bake in the oven for 3 hours. Remove from the oven and leave to cool, then crack the top open and scoop out the inside.

Heat the cream and butter gently. Blend the celeriac with cream and butter, pass through a sieve and season to taste.

For The Honey Soused Beetroot (Prepare at least 6 hours ahead)

Preheat the oven to 180°C (fan).

Bake your beetroots according to size until tender, peel while hot and set to one side. Sweat the shallots with the thyme, then *deglaze* with the sherry and vinegar. Add all other ingredients and reduce for a couple of minutes. Cut the beetroots into your desired shape. Marinate for at least 6 hours.

> **Chef's Tip**
>
> Make sure each type of beetroot is marinated separately to prevent bleeding into one another.

For The Spiced Venison

Fry the breadcrumbs in the oil until golden. Toast the juniper berries and peppercorns, grind, then add to breadcrumbs with the sea salt. Season and pan fry the venison for 5-6 minutes, allow to rest. Brush with the honey and roll in the spice mix.

For The Jus

Brown the bones and vegetables in a large pan. *Deglaze* with the port and Madeira. Add the stock and reduce to your preferred consistency. Once reduced sufficiently, season and pass through a fine sieve.

To Serve

Slice the venison, reheat the beetroot and purée. Assemble as pictured.

OUR BANOFFEE

SERVES 4

 Tokaji Noble Late Harvest
(Hungary)

Ingredients

Banana Cake
200g self-raising flour
1 tsp bicarbonate of soda
100g caster sugar
3 very ripe bananas (mashed)
120ml rapeseed oil
2 large eggs

Banana Sorbet
500g banana purée
150ml water
225g caster sugar
25g trimoline, 5g stabiliser
2 lemons (juice of)

Panna Cotta
300ml double cream
75ml whole milk
75g caster sugar
1 shot espresso
1 shot Kahlua
2 leaves gelatine (soaked in cold water)

Toffee Sauce
50g unsalted butter
100g caster sugar
25ml crème de banane
25ml double cream

Chocolate Soil
220g white sugar
75ml cold water
80g dark chocolate
25g maltodextrin
10ml hazelnut oil

To Serve
2 firm bananas
200ml whipping cream
50g icing sugar
1 vanilla pod (scraped), toffee shards

25cm x 12½cm baking tin (lined)
demitasse cups for the panna cotta (or you
could use an ice cube tray)

Method

For The Banana Cake
Preheat the oven to 155°C (fan).

Sieve the flour, sugar and bicarbonate of soda together.
Mix with the rest of the ingredients. Pour the batter into the
baking tin. Bake for 35 minutes or until a skewer comes out
clean. Leave to cool.

For The Banana Sorbet
Bring the sugar, water and stabiliser to the boil, then allow to
cool slightly. Stir in the purée, trimoline and lemon juice.
Chill, then pass through a sieve. Churn in an ice cream machine.
Store in the freezer.

For The Panna Cotta
Bring all the ingredients, except the gelatine, to the boil.
Remove from the heat and leave to cool. Whisk in the gelatine,
pass through a sieve, pour into moulds and set in fridge for
2-3 hours.

For The Toffee Sauce
Melt the sugar until it starts to caramelise. Stir in the cream,
butter and crème de banane.

For The Chocolate Soil
Bring the sugar and water to the boil and take to 135°C.
Take off the heat and whisk in the chocolate until caramelised.
Once cooled, blend with the maltodextrin and hazelnut oil.

To Serve
Whip the cream with the icing sugar and vanilla. Cut the cake
into squares and the bananas on an angle. Coat the cake and
bananas with toffee sauce and assemble as pictured with the
chocolate soil.

Chef's Tip
If your bananas are not ripe, freeze them. Once defrosted,
they will be perfect for purée.

102
THE EARL OF MARCH

Lavant Road, Chichester, West Sussex, PO18 0BQ

01243 533 993
www.theearlofmarch.com

The view from The Earl of March, across the undulating South Downs, inspired William Blake to write his ode to England's Green and Pleasant Land. The poet gazed upon the vista from the elevated vantage point before penning his Jerusalem.

Much has changed since Blake's time, but the sheer beauty of the west Sussex countryside has altered little. Visitors to The Earl of March, in Lavant, are able to drink in the rolling landscape as they relax amid comfortable surrounds.

Chef patron Giles Thompson cut his teeth as the executive chef at The Ritz and has brought élan and flair to The Earl of March. He acquired the venue seven years ago and has established it in the Michelin, Harden's and Good Food Guides. It is a cut above.

Standards are exceptionally high across the restaurant and bar, which serve the finest local food and drink.

The restaurant's culinary reputation is based on the use of exceptional West Sussex produce, including such seafood specialities as crab and lobster. The kitchen uses oysters and locally smoked fish, while there is a flavoursome game menu in season and plenty of locally reared meat from exceptional south coast suppliers.

"We take a real pride in what we do," says Giles. "Our customers expect the very best and that's what we work hard to deliver."

The venue is enviably situated in the heart of Goodwood, with the aerodrome, racecourse and motor circuit nearby.

Relish Restaurant Rewards
See page 003 for details.

Glorious Goodwood coupled with 'Food Glorious Food'
has given The Earl of March its recipe for success

CARAMELISED ONION TARTE TATIN, GOAT'S CHEESE ICE CREAM, HAZELNUT & PICKLED WALNUT SALAD, CARROT GEL

SERVES 4

 Glacier Park Sauvignon Blanc 2012 (New Zealand)

Ingredients

Caramelised Onion Tarte Tatin

250g red onions (thinly sliced)
65g dark brown sugar
1½g Maldon sea salt

Goat's Cheese Ice Cream (Makes 2 litres)

1kg goat's cheese
500ml double cream
250ml milk
250ml glucose syrup
6 leaves gelatine (soaked in cold water)
25ml vodka

Hazelnut And Pickled Walnut Salad

Pickled Walnuts:

65g walnut halves
35ml sweet cooking wine
35ml cider vinegar
Maldon sea salt (pinch of)
30g dark brown sugar
thyme (sprig of)
garlic (pinch of)
mace (pinch of)
1 star anise
3 juniper berries
1 bay leaf
5 peppercorns

Candied Hazelnuts:

65g whole hazelnuts (*blanched*)
35g caster sugar, 35g liquid glucose
65ml water

baby salad leaves

Carrot Gel

125ml carrot juice
3g ultratex

Method

For The Caramelised Onion Tarte Tatin

Melt the sugar in a heavy bottomed saucepan, then add the red onions. Bring to the boil, then reduce the heat to low. When the onion becomes translucent, the mix is ready. Strain off any liquid, add salt to taste, then chill.

> **Chef's Tip**
>
> The key to the flavours of the dish is how well the onions are caramelised, so be daring and give them plenty of colour.

For The Goat's Cheese Ice Cream

Heat the milk with the cream and melt in the goat's cheese. Stir in the gelatine and the glucose. Once dissolved, remove from the heat and add the vodka. Allow to cool, then churn in an ice cream machine. Store in the freezer when set.

For The Pickled Walnuts (Allow 24 hours)

Preheat the oven to 200°C.

Roast the walnut halves for 5 minutes.

Place all the remaining ingredients into a saucepan and boil for 5 minutes. Remove from the heat and add the walnuts. Leave to infuse for 24 hours before serving.

For The Candied Hazelnuts

Preheat the oven to 200°C.

Roast the hazelnuts for 5 minutes until golden.

Place the sugar, glucose and 1 tablespoon of the water into a heavy bottomed pan and boil. When it turns a deep caramel colour, add the rest of the water. Take care, sugar will bubble! Boil until all the sugar has dissolved, then pour in the roasted hazelnuts, stir and leave to cool.

Drain the walnuts and combine with the hazelnuts and baby salad leaves.

For The Carrot Gel

Combine the ingredients in a bowl and, using a hand blender, blend until it thickens. Pass through a *chinois* and decant into a squeezy bottle.

To Serve

Turn out the tarte tatin onto the serving plate and dress with the hazelnut and pickled walnut salad. Add a scoop of goat's cheese ice cream and finish with the carrot gel.

PAN FRIED LOIN OF VENISON, GOLDEN BEET PUREE, CELERIAC DAUPHINOISE, PORT & BLACKBERRY JUS, BUTTERED CURLY KALE

SERVES 4

 Boutinot Côtes du Rhône 2011
(France)

Ingredients

Pan Fried Loin Of Venison
4 x 170g venison loin
thyme (2 sprigs of)
1 tbsp olive oil
freshly ground black pepper

Golden Beet Purée
65g yellow beetroot
25ml water
Maldon sea salt
0.12g xanthan gum

Celeriac Dauphinoise
¼ celeriac
625g King Edward potatoes (peeled)
35ml cream, 35g butter
¼ shallot, ¼ clove garlic
rosemary (sprig of)
Maldon sea salt
freshly ground black pepper

Port And Blackberry Jus
100ml cooking port
150g blackberries
thyme (sprig of)
celery (stick of, diced)
1 carrot (diced)
500ml veal or beef stock
1 tbsp redcurrant jelly

Garnish
curly kale (buttered)
blackberries
yellow beets

10cm x 10cm tray (lined with parchment)

Method

For The Pan Fried Loin Of Venison (Allow 24 hours)

Marinate the venison in the olive oil, thyme and black pepper for 24 hours. Place in small vacuum pack bags and seal. Cook in a water bath at 54ºC and cook for 90 minutes. Alternatively, pan fry for 3-5 minutes and finish in the oven for 7 minutes at 180ºC. Allow to rest for 10 minutes.

> **Chef's Tip**
>
> We sous vide and precook our venison in a water bath which keeps it extremely tender.

For The Golden Beet Purée

Boil the beetroot, skin on, until tender. Plunge into an ice bath when cooked. Once cooled, peel and trim.

Put the beets in a blender and blend for 2½ minutes. While blending, add the water and xanthan gum. Season with salt to taste, then pass through a fine sieve.

For The Celeriac Dauphinoise

Slice the potatoes and celeriac as thinly as possible on a *mandolin*. Heat the cream and butter with all the other ingredients, remove from the heat and allow to infuse for 30 minutes. Strain the liquid onto the potatoes and celeriac. Mix well so it all gets coated, check the seasoning. Lay out on the prepared tray, then top with tin foil. Cook at 180ºC for 2 hours.

For The Port And Blackberry Jus

Sauté the celery with the carrot and thyme in a heavy bottomed saucepan until coloured. Add in the remaining ingredients and bring to the boil. Reduce until the stock is syrupy and glossy. The more the reduction, the stronger the *jus*. Pass through a fine sieve.

To Serve

Season and pan fry the venison in a little oil and butter for about 7 minutes. Heat the other components and arrange the purée and dauphinoise on a plate. Slice the venison in half crossways. Drizzle with the *jus* and garnish with the buttered kale, yellow beets and blackberries.

WHITE CHOCOLATE JELLY, SET LEMON CREAM, PISTACHIO BISCUIT, LEMON SORBET

SERVES 8

Passito Di Noto Planeta 2009
(Italy)

Ingredients

White Chocolate Jelly

400ml water
6 leaves gelatine (softened)
400g white chocolate

Set Lemon Cream

2 lemons (zest and juice of)
400ml double cream
165g caster sugar

Lemon Sorbet

350ml stock syrup
2 leaves gelatine (softened)
85g glucose syrup
350ml lemon juice

Pistachio Biscuit

30cm sheet rolled puff pastry
200g pistachios (crushed)
1 tbsp honey

Garnish

blackberries
popcorn
pistachios (crushed)

8 x ½ sphere moulds (6cm)

Method

For The White Chocolate Jelly

Boil the water and add the gelatine, stirring until dissolved. Remove from the heat and allow to cool slightly. Add the chocolate and whisk until combined. Pour into the sphere moulds and set for 4 hours in the fridge.

For The Set Lemon Cream (Prepare the day before)

Boil the cream with the sugar and lemon zest. Once boiled, remove from the heat and add the lemon juice.

Pour into a tub, cool, then set in the fridge overnight.

For The Lemon Sorbet

Bring all the ingredients to the boil in a pan and boil until they are all incorporated. Chill, then churn in an ice cream machine. Store in the freezer.

For The Pistachio Biscuit

Preheat the oven to 200°C.

Brush the pastry with the honey, then push the pistachios into the pastry. Place onto a tray lined with parchment and lay another layer of parchment on top, followed by another tray - this will stop the pastry rising. Bake for 30 minutes until golden. Allow to cool, then cut into rectangles, 2cm x 10cm.

To Serve

Serve as pictured.

> **Chef's Tip**
> Let everything breathe for a while so it is not stone cold - this will open up the flavours.

112
MATT GILLAN AT THE PASS

South Lodge Hotel, Brighton Road, Lower Beeding, Nr Horsham,
West Sussex, RH13 6PS

01403 891 711
www.southlodgehotel.co.uk Twitter: @MattGillan @SouthLodgeHotel

T he Pass opened its doors at South Lodge in 2008, amidst a significant reinvestment project that saw this captivating country house hotel grow from 45 to 89 bedrooms. The restaurant was refurbished in January 2015, reopening the brand new doors as 'Matt Gillan at The Pass'.

Based on the concept of 'The Chef's Table', the 26 seat restaurant is situated within the kitchen, with not one but three kitchen teams providing the backdrop. The scenery comes to life when Matt and his team deliver the award-winning dishes to the table, perfectly positioned to explain every ingredient, technique or inspiration on the plate.

Matt's focus on seasonal produce is offered through constantly evolving tasting menus. Ranging from four to 12 courses, the food reflects the unique environment of the restaurant, closing the rule book to restrictions to ensure guests have a dining experience to remember. From ingredients you perhaps wouldn't consider pairing together, to the sheer volume of techniques to bring the best flavour out of the produce, Matt and his brigade strive to keep each course interesting and tasty, whilst remaining very different from the last.

Restaurant manager, Tommaso de Cristofaro, ensures the creative vision also flows through the service team. Off piste wine pairings and intelligently created juices and infusions allow the front of house to be as interactive as the chefs in a way that enhances the food.

Relish Restaurant Rewards
See page 003 for details.

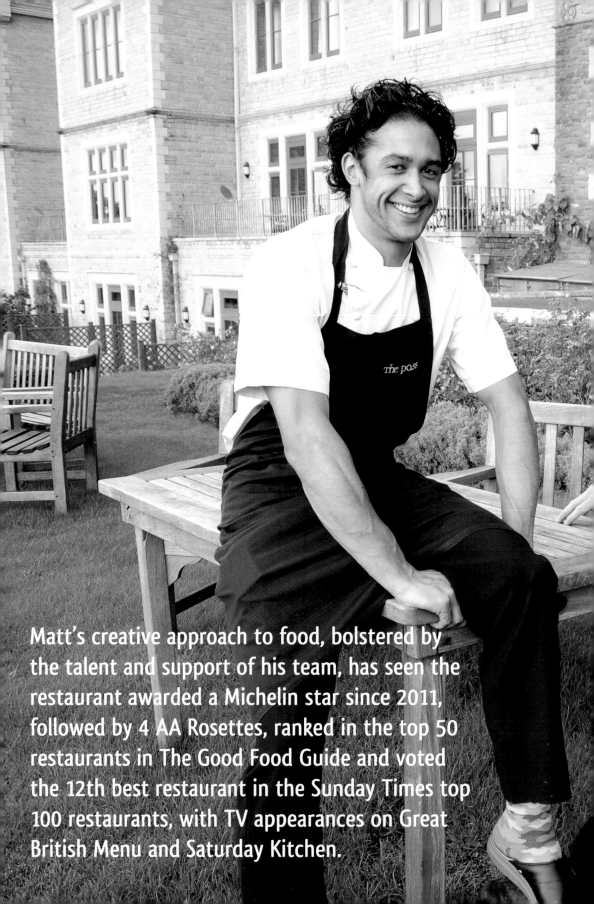

Matt's creative approach to food, bolstered by the talent and support of his team, has seen the restaurant awarded a Michelin star since 2011, followed by 4 AA Rosettes, ranked in the top 50 restaurants in The Good Food Guide and voted the 12th best restaurant in the Sunday Times top 100 restaurants, with TV appearances on Great British Menu and Saturday Kitchen.

OYSTER GLAZED CHICKEN THIGH, HOUMOUS, COFFEE

SERVES 4

Grüner Veltliner, 2012, Wachauer, Rainer Wess, Wachau (Austria)
A very new wine for which the first year of production was 2004. Reiner Wess always ensure optimal balance of ripeness and acidity; is crisp on the palate, mineral and mouth coating with a smoky finish which I believe would work very well with the particular flavour of the oyster sauce and in balance with the hint of coffee in the dish.

Ingredients

Chicken

4 chicken thighs (skin on, bone removed)
100ml good quality chicken stock
sea salt (flaked)
sunflower oil (for frying)

Oyster Sauce

200ml oyster sauce
200ml water
100ml brewed coffee

Houmous

250g tinned chickpeas (drained)
1 clove garlic (peeled, crushed to a paste)
100ml sesame oil
50g white sesame seeds (toasted)
50g black sesame seeds
1 lime (juice and zest of)
sunflower oil (if required)

Chickpeas

100g tinned chickpeas (drained, washed and dried)
1 tbsp Thai 7 spice
1 tbsp mild curry powder
1 tsp ground coffee
1 tsp salt
sunflower oil (for shallow frying)

Garnish

1 bunch watercress (picked)
2 tbsp freshly ground coffee powder

Method

For The Oyster Sauce

Mix all the ingredients together in a bowl.

For The Chicken

Heat a frying pan with a little sunflower oil on a high heat. Season the skin and place the thighs into the pan, skin-side down, and reduce to a medium heat. Cook until the skin is crisp and golden. Turn the thighs over, then add the chicken stock. Reduce heat to low and cook for 4-5 minutes until almost cooked. Remove from the heat and leave thighs in the stock until needed.

Drain off the stock and place the pan back on the heat. Add the oyster sauce and reduce to a nice glaze. Coat the chicken thighs generously.

> **Chef's Tip**
> Use good quality chicken to avoid water being released from the meat when frying the skin.

For The Houmous

Put all the ingredients, except the sesame seeds, into a food processor and blend. Add enough sunflower oil to achieve the required consistency. Add the sesame seeds and incorporate.

For The Chickpeas

Heat the oil to 180°C.

Combine the spices, salt and coffee, in a bowl.

Fry the chickpeas in the oil until the bubbles stop.

Remove and allow the excess oil to drain off. Tip the chickpeas into the spice mix and coat. Drain on kitchen paper.

To Assemble

Warm the houmous slightly and place a spoonful on a plate.

Place the thigh on top. Sprinkle crispy chickpeas over the chicken. Arrange watercress over and around, then finish with a dusting of coffee.

SALT BAKED PORK RUMP, ROASTED CARROTS, CORIANDER QUINOA, PESTO

SERVES 4-6

*Chardonnay, Honeycomb, Journey's End, 2009
(Stellenbosch, South Africa)
A very elegant Chardonnay, with almond and
brioche flavour given by the oak ageing of the wine.
Lovely balance of acidity and sweetness. Because of
its age, it has now developed enough richness to
pair with protein, the roasted carrots and the
nuttiness of the quinoa.*

Ingredients

Salt Dough

800g strong flour
300g table salt
6 egg whites
200ml water

The Pork

1 x 600-700g pork rump (skin removed,
fat left on)
1 clove garlic (sliced)
2 sprigs thyme

Coriander Quinoa

100g quinoa
300ml good quality chicken stock
20g butter
2 tbsp coriander (chopped)
30g Parmesan (finely grated)
salt (to taste)

Pesto

100g Parmesan (grated)
100g pine nuts (toasted)
200ml light olive oil
50g carrot tops (finely chopped)

Roasted Carrots

30 baby carrots, various colours
(reserve carrot tops)
100g butter
sunflower oil (for frying), salt

Sauce

50ml cassis, 150ml Madeira
1 litre good quality chicken stock
4 sundried tomatoes (finely chopped)

Method

For The Salt Dough

Mix the flour, salt and egg white together, then add the water to form a firm dough.

Roll out between greaseproof paper sheets to 3-4mm thick.

> **Chef's Tip**
>
> Play around with the aromats inside the dough with the pork.

For The Pork

Preheat the oven to 180°C (fan).

Place the garlic and thyme in the centre of dough. Arrange the rump, fat-side down, on top of the garlic. Pull the sides of dough together in the centre, ensuring it is tight and there are no gaps. Trim off any excess and fill any gaps with the dough trim.

Lay the pork on a greaseproof lined tray and bake in the oven for 28-35 minutes, depending on size.

Remove from the oven and allow to rest for 10 minutes.

Heat a frying pan with a little oil.

Open the crust, remove the garlic and thyme then place the rump, fat-side down, in the pan. Once coloured, turn, then continue to colour all around. Remove from the pan and rest for 10 minutes. Slice into 4-6 portions.

For The Coriander Quinoa

Preheat the oven to 180°C (fan).

Put the quinoa and chicken stock into an oven proof dish then cover. Transfer to the oven for 20 minutes.

Remove, stir in the butter, salt, Parmesan and coriander.

For The Pesto

Combine all the ingredients to create a chunky pesto.

For The Roasted Carrots

Preheat the oven to 180°C (fan).

Heat an ovenproof frying pan with a little oil.

Peel the carrots and add to the pan. Add the butter and place in the oven. Cook for 15-20 minutes until tender. Remove from oven. Season and sprinkle with the chopped carrot tops.

For The Sauce

Reduce the cassis and Madeira to a syrup. Add the chicken stock and reduce to a sauce consistency. Stir in the chopped tomatoes.

To Serve

Arrange your dish as pictured.

LEMON & GREEN TEA PARFAIT, YOGHURT SORBET, GREEN TEA MERINGUE

SERVES 6-8

*Beerenauslese, 2006, Dr Loosen (Mosel, Germany)
Wine produced with 100% Riesling grape only in
certain vintages, when the conditions are just right
for the development of botrytis. It has a very long
finish on the palate, gently sweet and not syrup
style with a slight hint of lemon to finish. This would
complement your fresh dessert perfectly giving a
very fresh finish on the palate.*

Ingredients

Green Tea Meringue

50g egg white (2-3 medium eggs)
50g icing sugar
50g caster sugar
10g Matcha green tea powder
extra Matcha green tea powder for dusting

Lemon And Green Tea Parfait

6 egg yolks
180g sugar
75ml water
1 lemon (fine zest and juice of)
20g Matcha green tea powder
300ml cream (whipped to firm peaks)

Yoghurt Sorbet

350ml water
200g sugar
600ml natural yoghurt
50g honey

Green Tea Jelly

300ml water
2 bags green tea
100g caster sugar
15g vegetable gelatine

Lemon Curd

5 egg yolks
1 egg
125g caster sugar
60ml lemon juice
50g butter

16 hemisphere moulds (5cm diameter x 3cm deep)

Method

Chef's Tip
Make everything a day in advance.

For The Green Tea Meringue
Preheat the oven to 100°C (fan).
Whisk the egg white in a stand up mixer until firm peaks form. Add the sugars and whisk until shiny. Whisk in the green tea.
Transfer to a piping bag. Line a tray with greaseproof paper and pipe lines down the length of the tray.
Cook in the oven for 1 hour, or until the meringue is crispy.
Allow 3 batons per person and crush any excess meringue for the parfait.

For The Lemon And Green Tea Parfait (Prepare ahead)
Whisk the egg yolks in a stand up mixer on full speed.
Bring the sugar and water to 121°C. Reduce the mixer speed and slowly add the sugar mix. Whisk on full until cool.
Add the lemon juice, zest and green tea powder. Mix well.
Fold into the whipped cream. Transfer to a piping bag and pipe into the hemisphere moulds.
Transfer to the freezer for at least 6 hours until firm.
Once firm, piece 2 halves together to form a sphere and roll in the broken meringue pieces.

For The Yoghurt Sorbet
Gently heat the sugar and water in a pan until the sugar dissolves.
Remove from the heat and add the honey. Allow to cool, then add to the yoghurt and mix well. Churn in an ice cream machine and transfer to the freezer.

For The Green Tea Jelly
Bring the water to the boil. Remove from the heat and add the tea bags. Allow to infuse for 4 minutes, then remove the tea bags.
Add the sugar and gelatine to the tea and whisk together.
Return to the heat and bring back to the boil. Pour into a small container and leave to set. Cut into ½cm cubes.

For The Lemon Curd
Whisk all ingredients together, except the butter. Place the bowl over a pan of simmering water and whisk until light and fluffy.
Remove from the heat and whisk in the butter. Transfer to a new bowl to prevent over cooking.

To Serve
Dust a line of finely powdered meringue across the centre of the plate. Place a parfait ball, a scoop of the sorbet and the piped meringue batons along the line. Finish with the jelly cubes and lemon curd.

122
OCKENDEN MANOR HOTEL & SPA

Cuckfield, West Sussex, RH17 5LD

01444 416 111
www.hshotels.co.uk/ockenden-manor-hotel-and-spa/dining
Twitter: @OckendenManor Facebook: Ockenden Manor

Michelin starred fine dining, sumptuous afternoon teas and one of the UK's finest spas are among the attractions at Ockenden Manor Hotel and Spa.

The charming and tranquil Elizabethan manor house is tucked away in Cuckfield, one of the prettiest Tudor villages in England.

With its history and character, elegant sitting room warmed by a roaring log fire and cosy, wood panelled bar, it's a wonderful place to escape to.

Set in nine acres of peaceful gardens and parkland with views across the West Sussex countryside to the South Downs, it is within easy reach of London and some of the great gardens and stately homes of Sussex and Kent.

Guests are assured of a warm welcome by general manager Adam Smith and his team and the very best of hospitality and cuisine, which has been recognised by AA and Michelin awards.

Head chef Stephen Crane leads the Michelin starred restaurant at Ockenden Manor, which offers a superb fine dining experience. A beautiful, new dining room overlooks the gardens, with stunning views of the South Downs National Park.

Crane is a sublime cook and serves some of the finest food in southern England. He incorporates the freshest ingredients sourced locally in Sussex, whenever possible.

Guests have a choice of fixed price menus, including Stephen's selected Cuckfield Menu, or the gastronomic seven course Tasting Menu, which focuses on the best of modern British and modern French cuisine. An inspired wine list complements the experience.

Relish Restaurant Rewards
See page 003 for details.

Lunch and dinner are not the only crowd pleasers. Ockenden Manor offers one of the region's most extravagant and tempting afternoon teas, before roaring log fires in autumn and winter, or on a stunning terrace in spring and summer.

HOME SMOKED MACKEREL, ASSIETTE OF BEETROOT, HORSERADISH, OYSTER CRACKERS

SERVES 4

 Sauvignon Blanc, Turning Heads, 2013 (New Zealand)

Ingredients

Mackerel
4 mackerel fillets (pin boned, skin on)
125g rock salt
8 juniper berries
2 tbsp black peppercorns
1 sprig rosemary
2 tbsp coriander seeds
2 bay leaves
100g Demerara sugar

Beetroot Purée
2 large red beetroot (finely diced)
1 sprig thyme, 1 clove garlic (crushed)

Pickled And Smoked Beetroot
1 large golden beetroot
1 candied beetroot
1 tsp black peppercorns
1 tsp juniper berries
½ tsp cloves, 3 star anise
500ml water
500ml white wine vinegar
250g sugar, 1 tbsp salt
1 sprig thyme, 1 bay leaf

Horseradish Cream
100ml double cream
1 tbsp horseradish sauce
lemon juice (spritz of)
salt (pinch of)
dill and parsley (finely chopped)

Oyster Crackers
3 fresh oysters (including juice)
50ml chicken stock
50g tapioca flour

Garnish
apple batons, seasonal leaves

Method

For The Mackerel
Combine the herbs, spices and 25g of the rock salt and blend together in a thermomix until a fine dust - around 3 minutes. Mix with the remaining rock salt and Demerara sugar. Line a container with a little of the marinade and place in the mackerel fillets, skin-side down. Cover the top of the mackerel in the remaining marinade. Cover with cling film and refrigerate for 2 hours. Wash the marinade off and rinse the fish in running water for 5 minutes to remove the salt. Place on a dry towel and pat off any moisture. Transfer to a smoker for 3 hours. Once smoked, cook the mackerel in an oven at 160°C (fan) for around 3-5 minutes, until the flesh is just cooked. Cool in the fridge, then pick large flakes, discarding the skin.

Chef's Tip
To debone the mackerel, run a knife either side of the bone and pull it out. If you don't have a smoker, buy the fish already smoked.

For The Beetroot Purée
Place all the ingredients into a pan, just cover with water and simmer until cooked through. Drain through a sieve into another pan, squeezing as much liquid out as possible. Blitz the cooked beetroot until smooth, then pass through a *chinois*. Reduce the strained liquid to a syrup, stir into the purée and season.

For The Pickled And Smoked Beetroot
Toast the spices in a hot pan for 1 minute to release the oils. Add in all the other ingredients and bring to the boil to dissolve the sugar. Simmer for 10 minutes, then remove from the heat. Once cool, pass through a sieve. Boil the beets in a pan of salted water until a knife can go through easily. Cool before peeling. Slice the golden beetroot on a *mandolin* and place in the pickling *liquor*. Marinate for 2 hours. Cut the candied beetroot into 1cm dice. Place in a smoker for 25 minutes before using.

For The Horseradish Cream
Whisk the double cream with the horseradish sauce until stiff peaks form. Add the lemon juice, salt and herbs to taste.

For The Oyster Crackers
Combine all ingredients in a thermomix and set to 90°C. Cook at speed 5 for 25 minutes. Spread thinly over a silpat mat and dry overnight at 55°C. Once dry, break into pieces and deep fry at 190°C until they puff up.

To Serve
Plate as pictured.

BALCOME ESTATE DUCK BREAST, STUFFING, PUMPKIN, APPLE, HAZELNUT, BROCCOLI

SERVES 4

 Deen De Bortoli, Vat 10, Pinot Noir, 2011 (Australia)

Ingredients

Duck

1 whole duck (legs and breasts removed, bones reserved)
2 bulbs garlic and 2 handfuls mixed herbs (both roughly chopped) mixed with 4 handfuls coarse sea salt
duck fat (to *confit*)
1 tbsp honey (for the breast)

Duck Stuffing

1 shallot (finely chopped)
1 clove garlic (finely chopped)
butter (knob of)
4 duck livers (finely chopped, sinew removed)
2 slices white bread (crusts removed, diced, soaked in milk to soften)
handful parsley (finely chopped)
2 eggs
confit duck leg meat (reserved from earlier)

Pumpkin Purée

100g butter
2 sprigs rosemary
¼ large pumpkin (peeled, seeds removed)

Roasted Pumpkin

30g butter
2 sprigs thyme
¾ pumpkin (cut into segments)
salt (pinch of), sugar (pinch of)
2 cloves garlic
2 tbsp oil
2 tbsp hazelnuts (toasted, chopped)

Caramelised Apple

1 tbsp caster sugar, melted to a caramel, then tossed with 5g butter and 1 Granny Smith apple (cut into 16cm x 1cm dice)

To Serve

8 spears tenderstem broccoli (boiled), then griddled with butter and seasoned with salt

Method

For The Confit Duck Legs (Allow 36 hours)

Sprinkle half of the herb and garlic salt in a container, lay the legs on top and cover with the remaining salt. Lay a damp tea towel on top, then another container and weigh it down to press the legs. Press in the fridge for 24 hours.

Remove the legs and wash in a sink of running water for 20 minutes. Place the legs in a pan and cover with duck fat. *Confit* for 8 hours at 90°C (fan). Remove the legs from the fat and remove the skin. Pick through the meat and discard any bones. Finely chop the leg meat.

> **Chef's Tip**
> When cooking the duck breast, place a plate on top of it to keep it flat and to get the skin crispy.

For The Duck Stuffing

Sweat the shallots and garlic in butter until soft, add the livers and cook through. Squeeze the milk from the bread and combine all the ingredients together. Season well, roll into a sausage shape and wrap in cling film. Simmer in a pan for 30 minutes, then leave to cool in the water. Cut into 2cm slices and remove the cling film. Fry the slices on both sides until golden.

For The Pumpkin Purée

Preheat the oven to 180°C (fan).
Cook the butter and rosemary in a pan on a low heat until it turns golden brown (*noisette*). Pass through a fine muslin. Wrap the pumpkin tightly in foil and roast for 1 hour until soft. Place in a sieve over a pan and squeeze out any water from the pumpkin. Blitz the pumpkin with the butter until smooth, then pass through a *chinois*. Reduce the strained liquid to a syrup, add this back to the purée and season.

For The Roasted Pumpkin

Preheat the oven to 200°C (fan).
Place the pumpkin segments on a baking tray with the garlic, 1 sprig of thyme, salt, sugar, half the oil and half the butter. Cover the tray with foil and bake until extremely soft, but still holding its shape - about 20-25 minutes.
Place in a hot pan with the remaining oil, colour on both sides, then remove from the heat and add the remaining ingredients.

For The Duck Breast

Score the skin and place skin-side down in a hot pan. Once golden and crispy, turn over and seal all sides of the breasts, then remove from the pan. Wipe the pan clean and caramelise the honey. Drop the breasts, skin-side down, in the honey and coat. Take out and leave to rest for 5 minutes before slicing. Serve as pictured.

WARM PEAR FRITTER, PEAR SALAD, SALTED CARAMEL ICE CREAM

SERVES 4

 *The Pilot, Late Harvest Semillon
(New Zealand)*

Ingredients

Pear Fritter

4 pears (peeled, cored, diced)
50g butter
sweet mixed spice (to taste)
caster sugar (to taste)
1 tbsp flour mixed with 1 tbsp water
4 sheets feuille de brick pastry
handful raisins (soaked in boiling water)
icing sugar (to dust)

Salted Caramel Ice Cream

200g Demerara sugar
50ml maple syrup
50g unsalted butter
12 egg yolks
50g caster sugar
570ml full-fat milk
190ml double cream
½ vanilla pod
2 tsp fleur de sel
25g trimoline

Pear Salad

2 pears
½ cinnamon stick
½ star anise
honey, caster sugar, water (all to taste)

Milk Chocolate Caramel

80g caster sugar
10g butter
290ml double cream
8g glucose syrup
90g 40% milk chocolate (melted)

To Serve

Boiron pear purée

Method

For The Pear Fritter (Prepare the day before)

Melt the butter, then add the pears, spice and sugar. Cook on a low heat until the pear is soft, but holds its shape. Squeeze the raisins and add to the pear. Combine the flour and water to make a paste. Take 1 sheet of feuille de brick and place a quarter of the mixture in a line, just below the middle of the pastry. Lightly brush the flour paste on the top half and to the sides. Fold over the bottom half tightly, then fold the 2 sides towards each other and stick. Roll upwards to create a spring roll shape.

Deep fry at 190°C until golden. Dust with icing sugar.

> **Chef's Tip**
>
> Prepare the pear mix the day before and wrap in cling film in a sausage shape – this will make it easier to roll.

For The Salted Caramel Ice Cream (Make the day before)

In a food processor, mix the Demerara sugar for 1 minute, then add the maple syrup, butter and trimoline. Heat in a pan for 30 minutes, then add the fleur de sel.

Whisk the egg yolks and sugar to make a *sabayon*. Bring the milk, cream and vanilla pod to the boil. Remove from the heat and add the *sabayon* whilst whisking. Place back on the heat to 85°C. Stir together and cool in a tub surrounded by ice. Leave to infuse overnight, then churn in an ice cream machine.

For The Pear Salad

Peel, core and quarter 1 pear. In a deep pan, place the cinnamon, star anise, honey, caster sugar and water. Mix together and add the pear. Place a *cartouche* on top. Bring to a simmer and cook until the pear is soft but still with shape. Dice half of the remaining pear into cubes and the other half into batons.

Milk Chocolate Caramel

In a heavy bottomed pan, heat the sugar, without stirring, until it turns into a caramel. Remove from the heat, then add the butter. Boil the cream and glucose, then pour both mixtures over the melted chocolate and combine.

To Serve

Using a bottle, zig zag the milk chocolate caramel across the plate. Trim the ends of the fritter and cut in the middle at an angle. Plate standing up. Dot the pear purée up one side with the diced pear at the base. Cut the poached pear into 4 and arrange next to the purée. Stand some of the pear batons on top of the poached pear. Finally, *quenelle* the ice cream and place on top of the diced pear.

132
THE RESTAURANT AT DRAKES

43-44 Marine Parade, Brighton, BN2 1PE

01273 696 934
www.therestaurantatdrakes.co.uk Twitter @DrakesRest

The subterranean fine dining restaurant where Andy MacKenzie plies his trade is one of the south east's best kept secrets.

The Restaurant at Drakes, on Brighton's Marine Parade, serves muscular, big-hearted dishes that max out on flavour. MacKenzie is a classy customer, whose artistry enables him to create plates that are easy on the eye.

Drakes is within sight of the iconic beach where mods and rockers fought in the movie Quadrophenia. A contemporary edge runs through its cocktail lounge, where visitors can kick back and enjoy sundowners within a stone's throw of the seashore.

Downstairs, MacKenzie welcomes customers into the 36 cover restaurant. His reputation is spreading quickly, thanks to listings in the Michelin Guide, Harden's and the Good Food Guide.

MacKenzie has an impressive CV that includes stints at Gleneagles, at Chez Nico 90 Park Lane and Mossiman's Belfry in London, as well as further afield in Australia and beyond.

MacKenzie says: "I started out near Birmingham and travelled the world before arriving at Drakes.

"Being well travelled broadened my horizons and helped to expand my repertoire.

"I had a year in Australia, cooking Moroccan food, which I really enjoyed. I'm happily established here at Drakes. I opened the restaurant 10 years ago and we're really hitting our stride."

Drakes' menu is seasonal and local. MacKenzie is well connected with farmers who supply him with Dexter beef and Gloucester Old Spot. Gamekeepers keep him in pheasant, fishermen provide the freshest catch and fruit and vegetables are picked and delivered within 24 hours.

"It's a beautiful location." 'Beautiful' describes the food too.

Relish Restaurant Rewards
See page 003 for details.

For over 10 years, Andy and his loyal team have been preparing excellent food at The Restaurant at Drakes, coupled with outstanding service from Radka, the restaurant manager and Eddy, the sommelier.

SCALLOPS WITH PEA PUREE

SERVES 4

 Bluebell Vineyard Estate Hindleap Blanc de Blancs (England)

Ingredients

Scallops

8 large hand-dived scallops
butter (knob of)
½ lemon (seeds removed)

8 thin slices pancetta

Pea Foam And Purée

500g frozen peas
2 banana shallots (sliced)
4 cloves garlic (sliced)
1 litre vegetable stock (hot)
15g soya lecithin
butter (knob of)

Salad

1 head frisée lettuce (picked)
1 firm sour apple (cut into matchsticks)
2 tbsp lemongrass dressing

Method

For The Scallops

Carefully open the scallops and remove the skirt. Wash in cold water and store in the fridge, flat-side down.

For The Pea Foam And Purée

Sauté the shallot and garlic gently in a pan, without colouring, until translucent. Add the peas and cover with vegetable stock, simmer for 2 minutes, then remove from the heat. Pass off the liquid and retain for the foam.

Add a third of the peas to the liquid and blend in a thermo mixer. Stir in the soya lecithin (about 15g per litre) and taste for seasoning. Pass through a fine sieve and cool over ice.

Take the remaining peas and blend in a thermo mixer to a very fine purée. Season and pass through a fine *chinois*. Cool over iced water.

For The Pancetta

Preheat the oven to 160°C (fan).

Place the pancetta between 2 sheets of non-stick paper on a heavy baking tray with another tray on top. Cook in the oven, checking every 5 minutes, until they are crisp and golden brown. Remove and cool on a rack.

To Finish The Dish

Cook the scallops in a hot non-stick frying pan, service-side down, until they turn golden brown. Turn over, add a little bit of butter and cook for a further 2 minutes. Squeeze in the lemon, remove from the pan and rest on a cloth.

Heat the pea purée in a pan and add a little bit of butter.

Place a dollop of pea purée on the left side of the plate and, with a cranked palette knife, spread to the right. Place the scallops on the purée with a gap between them. Dress the salad and put between. Rest the pancetta on the salad.

Heat the retained pea liquid to 50°C, then hand blend with the container at a slight angle to allow foam to form on the surface. Rest it for 30 seconds to allow the liquid to fall from the foam, then spoon the foam on top of the scallops.

Chef's Tip

I like to use a flat, slate plate for this dish. It looks amazing!

ROAST PARTRIDGE

SERVES 4

 *Bluebell Vineyard Estate Hindleap Classic Cuvée
2010 (England)*

Ingredients

Partridges

4 whole partridges (*New York dressed*)
4 cloves garlic (whole)
5 sprigs thyme
butter (knob of)
brandy (splash of)
4 slices Alsace bacon
small piece *crépinette*

Partridge Sauce

reserved bones (from the partridges)
4 shallots (sliced)
6 cloves garlic (sliced)
½ bottle dry white wine
2 litres veal stock

Bread Sauce

4 slices bread (crust removed, diced)
285ml milk
1 shallot (studded with 4 cloves)
1 shallot (diced)
butter (knob of)

To Serve

100g emmer wheat (*blanched* in salted water)
2 William pears (peeled, cored, cut into 6 pieces
and roasted in butter until golden brown)
8 stems tenderstem broccoli (*blanched*
and chilled)
butter, salt and pepper

Bluebell Vineyard Estate wines, see page 214

Method

For The Partridge

Remove the legs from the partridges and set to one side. Remove the wishbones and the guts, reserving the livers. Next, cut out the backbones and reserve with the wishbones.

Put a clove of garlic and a sprig of thyme into each crown with a knob of butter, then vacuum seal, individually, in bags.

Remove the meat from 4 of the partridge legs. *Blanch* the feet of the other 4 legs in boiling water and pull off the skin with a cloth. Remove the thigh and shin bone, but leave the foot attached.

Combine the livers and leg meat with the diced shallot and fry in a hot pan. Add the brandy, then remove from the heat. Chop with a knife and place into a piping bag.

Lay the partridge legs flat, skin-side down with the cavity open. Pipe a little of the liver mix into the gap, then roll in the Alsace bacon and wrap in the *crépinette*, making sure there are no holes. Rest in the fridge.

For The Partridge Sauce

Fry the partridge bones in a heavy pan. Add the shallots and garlic and cook until golden brown. Add the white wine and reduce it slightly, then add the veal stock and reduce the whole lot by about half. Keep skimming until it reaches sauce consistency. Pass several times through a muslin cloth.

For The Bread Sauce (Prepare ahead)

Simmer the milk with the clove studded shallot for 2 minutes. Remove from the heat and leave to stand for 2 hours. Pass through a sieve.

In a separate pan, sweat the diced shallot in a little butter, add the bread and cover with the milk. Cook for 5 minutes, then blend in a thermo mix and pass through a sieve.

To Finish

Put the partridge in a water bath at 64°C for 20 minutes. At the same time, fry the leg parcels on both sides and place into a hot oven (200°C fan) for 4 minutes, then remove and rest.

Remove from the water bath and dry with a towel. Fry in a pan until golden brown on all sides, then remove from the pan and rest.

Put the emmer wheat into a pan and cook with some of the partridge sauce until soft and tender.

Heat the bread sauce and partridge sauce, checking for seasoning.

Remove the breasts from the partridge and cut the bottom off the leg parcel to allow it to stand.

Place 2 lines of the bread sauce purée on each plate with a spoonful of emmer wheat. Place the leg standing up, with the foot in the air. Dress with the roast pear. Sit the breast on the emmer wheat. Heat up the broccoli in a little butter, then add this to the plate. Spoon on a little partridge sauce and serve the rest in a jug.

PASSION FRUIT SOUFFLE

SERVES 4

 Bluebell Vineyard Estate Hindleap Rosé Brut (England)

Ingredients

Passion Fruit Jam

500g passion fruit purée
250g sugar
1 lemon (juice of)

Passion Fruit Sauce

6 passion fruit
100g sugar
a little water

Vanilla Ice Cream

500ml whipping cream
1 vanilla pod
100g sugar
2.5g cremador

Soufflé

200g egg whites (from 5-6 eggs)
½ lemon (juice of)

Crème Pâtissière

1.1 litres milk
500g sugar
6-8 egg yolks (depending on the size of eggs)
200g plain flour

To Finish

icing sugar (to dust)

4 soufflé moulds (4½cm deep, 9cm diameter, greased with 5g soft butter and 2 tbsp caster sugar for coating)

Method

For The Passion Fruit Jam

Mix the passion fruit purée with the sugar and lemon juice and bring to the boil. Cook until it reaches setting point. Set aside.

For The Passion Fruit Sauce

Remove the passion fruit flesh from the shell, add the sugar and a little water and simmer for 4 minutes until syrupy.

For The Vanilla Ice Cream

Heat the cream, then add the vanilla pod and sugar. Simmer for 1 minute, then add the cremador. Simmer for a further 2 minutes, then freeze in a Pacojet container to -30°C.

Blend in the Pacojet 15 minutes before serving.

For The Crème Pâtissière

Bring the milk to a simmer. Whisk the egg yolks, flour and sugar together. Pour the milk over the egg mixture and whisk. Return to the heat and cook out gently. Put to one side, then weigh into 220g portions.

For The Soufflé

Preheat the oven to 180°C (fan).

Brush the ramekins with the soft butter to form a light, even coating on the inside of each dish. Pour the sugar into the first ramekin. Hold over the second ramekin and turn slowly so the entire inside is coated with the sugar. Once complete, pour the excess sugar into the second ramekin and repeat until all 4 ramekins are buttered and sugared.

Whisk the egg whites and lemon juice until light and fluffy.

Mix the jam with the custard.

Whisk one third of the egg white into the custard. Mix well, then fold in the rest of the egg whites with care.

Pour into the prepared soufflé moulds and cook in the oven for 10 minutes.

Dust with fine icing sugar.

To Serve

Serve immediately with passion fruit sauce and vanilla ice cream.

Chef's Tip

The best way to eat the soufflé is to make a hole with your spoon in the middle, place the ice cream inside and pour the passion fruit sauce on top. Enjoy!

142
TERRE à TERRE

71 East Street, Brighton, BN1 1HQ

01273 729 051
www.terreaterre.co.uk Twitter: @TerreaTerre

Long before vegetarianism became fashionable, there was Amanda Powley and Philip Taylor.

The pioneering business partners met in a subterranean kitchen and, recognising in each other a kindred spirit, they embarked upon a venture that would change the face of British gastronomy.

Their Terre à Terre restaurant was founded as a 28 seat café and quickly evolved into a 110 cover restaurant. It rapidly became a culinary destination, breaking the mould and confounding preconceived ideas about vegetarian food.

The winner of multiple awards, Terre à Terre is all about indulgence rather than abstinence. It has been feeding loyal customers and international visitors for more than 20 years. Diners enjoy a culinary experience like no other, with intense flavours, sublime textures and a mixture of ingredients that few have the imagination or would dare to compose. Put simply, Terre à Terre serves a symphony of harmonic flavours.

Head chef Matty Bowling is a firm believer that there are no limits to what the humble vegetable, root, fungi, seed, herb, flower, fruit and nut can deliver. Inspired by the likes of Rene Redzepi, Ben Shewry and David Chang, he trained in his native New Zealand and travelled the world before arriving on the South Coast.

His team's starry flavour is complemented by an extensive and organic vegetarian wine list and a full range of retail products. A committed, knowledgeable and engaging front of house team complete the experience.

During its 'two decade and then some' tenure, Terre à Terre has become both an icon and an institution. All things Brighton beautiful.

Relish Restaurant Rewards
See page 003 for details.

Acknowledged for its groundbreaking culinary combinations and top service, Terre à Terre has been listed in the Michelin and AA Guides since 2001 and won numerous local and national awards over the years.

OYSTER ORZOTTO

SERVES 4-6

Fiano, Feudo di Santa Tresa, 2013 (v)
(Sicily, Italy)

Ingredients

Almond Soup

100g blanched almonds
2 cloves garlic
40ml olive oil
340ml water
18ml white wine vinegar
2g salt

Artichoke Cream

500g Jerusalem artichoke (peeled, chopped)
½ white onion
10g butter
260ml full-fat milk
25ml cream
2 cloves garlic

Pearl Barley Risotto

4 shallots (chopped)
250g pearl barley
½ tsp lemon thyme
150ml white wine
700ml vegetable stock
olive oil (for frying)
½ tbsp lemon olive oil (optional)

Potato Crisps

1 large potato
vegetable oil (for frying)
salt
sumac

To Assemble

6 king oyster mushrooms
10ml olive oil
15g butter

Garnish

baby red chard

Method

For The Almond Soup

Blitz the almonds in a blender to form a smooth paste. Add the garlic, olive oil and half the water. In a slow, steady stream, add the rest of the water until the mixture is smooth with the consistency of cream. Finally, add the vinegar and season to taste.

For The Artichoke Cream

Melt the butter in a pan over a low heat. Add the onion and cook for 5 minutes. Next, add the artichoke and cook for 3 minutes. Stir in the milk and cream, then the garlic. Cook until soft. Blend in a mixer until smooth. Taste and season. Pass the sauce through a fine sieve.

For The Pearl Barley Risotto

Cook the shallots with the olive oil until soft. Add the barley and thyme and cook for 2 minutes. Stir in the white wine and cook until the liquid is reduced. Pour in the stock and cook all until 90% of the liquid is absorbed. The barley should be just soft to the bite. To finish the risotto, add the artichoke cream, a little at a time, until you reach a desired consistency.

> **Chef's Tip**
> When finishing pearl barley, add ½ tablespoon of lemon olive oil for extra flavour.

For The Potato Crisps

Slice the potatoes about 0.75cm thick (a *mandolin* helps). Rinse under cold water until the water runs clear. Drain well and pat dry. Deep fry the potatoes, in 6 batches, in oil at 160°C, turning occasionally to cook evenly, until golden brown and crisp. Transfer to a wire rack lined with a paper towel. Season with salt and sumac.

To Assemble

Preheat the oven to 180°C.

Season the mushrooms with olive oil, salt and pepper. Pan fry in butter then finish in the oven for 6 minutes, turning once. Slice into 3 rounds. Spoon the almond soup onto a plate, place a portion of risotto in the centre and place the 3 rounds of mushrooms on top. Finish with potato crisps and garnish with seasoned baby red chard if available.

BETTER BATTER

SERVES 4-6

🍷 *Riesling Trocken Qualitätswein Weingut zur*
Römerkelter, 2012/13 (v) (Mosel, Germany)

Ingredients

Yemen Paste

230g hot, red chillies (chopped)
5 cloves garlic
¼ tbsp black peppercorns
½ tsp coriander seeds
65g coriander (leaves and stalks)
½ tsp salt
150ml olive oil (plus extra for topping up)

Lemony Yemeni Pickle

3 lemons (peel and pith removed,
flesh cut into segments)
100ml lemon juice
3 preserved lemons (peel of), 150g caster sugar
½ tsp yemen paste (to taste, see above)

Sea Salad Tartare Sauce

1 nori sheet (dried seaweed), 40g parsley
100g capers (rinsed), 100g gherkins (rinsed)
100g thai pink shallots, 150ml mayonnaise

Minty Mushy Peas

400g fresh or frozen peas
40g mint and 40g parsley (leaves and stalks
separated, leaves chopped)
50g unsalted butter
salt, freshly ground black pepper

Chip Shop Batter

150g plain flour, 75g self-raising flour
10ml white wine vinegar, 240ml cold water
½ tsp baking powder
salt and freshly ground black pepper

Buttermilk Soaked Halloumi

500g halloumi cheese (2 packs of 250g)
500ml buttermilk (or 250ml yoghurt mixed with
250ml milk)
plain flour (for coating)
sunflower oil (for deep frying)

To Assemble

3 lemons (halved, griddled)
2 tbsp mint (chopped)
3 cooked/pickled quail eggs (cut in half)

Method

For The Yemen Paste

Liquidise all the ingredients together in a jug blender until they form a paste.

For The Lemony Yemeni Pickle

Blend half the lemon flesh, juice and peel together at high speed in a blender or food processor. Place in a small pan with the sugar, stir and heat gently. Boil rapidly for 2 minutes. Add the yemen paste according to your taste. Leave to cool and add the remaining segments.

For The Sea Salad Tartare Sauce

Hold the nori sheet briefly over a flame to heat both sides - for no more than 2 seconds or it will burn. Finely chop all the ingredients and bind with mayonnaise.

For The Minty Mushy Peas

Cook the peas with the herb stalks until tender in boiling water. Drain well, discarding the stalks. Blend the peas with the butter and herbs. Season to taste.

For The Chip Shop Batter

Whisk all the ingredients together to create a batter to the consistency of double cream. Keep refrigerated until you are ready to coat and fry the halloumi.

For The Buttermilk Soaked Halloumi (Prepare the day before)

Carefully cut the halloumi into thin triangles. Submerge the cheese in the buttermilk and leave to soak in the refrigerator for several hours or overnight. Just before serving, drain the halloumi, dip in plain flour and then in the batter. Deep fry at 180°C, 2 pieces at a time, until crisp and golden brown. Drain on paper towels.

To Plate

Divide the halloumi between the plates, top with a spoonful of the pickle. Add the warm mushy peas. Finish with sea salad tartare, and garnish with half a griddled lemon and half a pickled quail egg.

Chef's Tip

Test your fryer oil temperature with a cube of bread, if it turns brown in a minute it's ready.

KULFI CONE & BRIGHTON BEACH BOONDI POPS

SERVES 4-6

Moscato d'Asti, DOCG, Piedmont, 2013 (v)
(Italy)

Ingredients

Kulfi Custard

3 litres full-fat milk
180g caster sugar
1 bay leaf
½ tsp ground cardamom
¼ tsp cinnamon
¼ tsp salt, ¼ tsp pepper
saffron strands (2 pinches of)
150g mix of almonds and pistachios
(toasted, then ground)
1 tsp rosewater

The Boondi

300g gram flour, 250ml water
oil (for deep frying)

Boondi Sauce

100g sugar
20ml water
40g butter
110ml orange juice
30ml lemon juice
10g orange zest
50ml Cointreau, 30ml brandy

Poppy Seed Cones

100ml water
250g sugar, 50g glucose
30g unsalted butter, 80g plain flour
2 tbsp poppy seeds (to sprinkle)

Coconut Lime Yoghurt

1 lime (juice and zest of) combined with
250g coconut yoghurt

To Finish

flaked almonds, toasted pistachios
passion fruit, pomegranate molasses
edible flowers

kulfi cone moulds

Method

For The Kulfi Custard (Prepare the day before)

Start by making evaporated milk. Boil 1 litre of milk over a medium heat, stir continuously until reduced to the consistency of thick batter. Boil the remaining 2 litres of milk with the sugar and bay leaf, stirring periodically. When reduced by half, add everything else, apart from the evaporated milk, and continue to cook for 10 minutes. Add the evaporated milk, then stir. Leave the custard in the fridge overnight then strain through a sieve. The custard can be set in the freezer. To get the cone effect use kulfi cone moulds, line them with parchment and pour the custard into them. Stand them upright in the freezer to set.

Chef's Tip

To make things easier (and to avoid cones), set the kulfi in a large tray and portion to suit. Break up the poppy seed sugar sheets into shards.

For The Boondi

Heat about 5cm of oil in a deep pan. Whisk together both ingredients to make a batter. Pour the batter through a slotted spoon and deep fry until the droplets are golden brown. Remove and place onto a tea towel to drain off the excess oil.

For The Boondi Sauce

Bring the sugar and water to a caramel (160°C) in a heavy bottomed saucepan, then whisk in the butter. Add the juices and zest, stirring and reduce the mix by a third. Add the alcohol and bring back to the boil.

For The Poppy Seed Cones

Bring the water, sugar and glucose to the boil, whisk in the butter, then add the flour. Set in the fridge for 1-2 hours until cold. Spread the mix thinly onto a silicone mat, then sprinkle with poppy seeds. Bake the sheets at 220°C for 10 minutes until completely golden brown. While warm, transfer to a chopping board and cut into circles using a round cutter. In a low oven (140°C), warm up the circles and wrap them around the metal cone moulds. Leave until completely cooled.

To Assemble

Place the kulfi ice inside the poppy seed cone and position on the plate, cone pointing up. Heat the boondi sauce, fold through the boondi and some toasted pistachios and flaked almonds. Spoon around the cone. Add a spoonful of coconut lime yoghurt and finish with fresh passion fruit, pomegranate molasses and edible flowers, if available.

KENT & SURREY
HOME GROWN QUALITY

Introduction by Richard Phillips, Chef/Owner Thackeray's, Pearsons Arms & The Windmill

Few counties can boast the variety or quality of ingredients which can be found in Kent and Surrey. With such a fabulous array of arable produce complemented by livestock and increasingly great beers and wines, the choice for chefs to demonstrate their culinary skills is truly awesome.

Like all good chefs, I rely on quality ingredients, the fresher the better, so with our proximity to the sea and rich farmland, the food in our restaurants is surely second to none.

I began my career at Thanet College and have continued supporting this establishment ever since. It taught me the values of simplicity which, of course, is the main tenet of chefs around the world. The greatest achievement for me and others is passing on experience of the professional kitchen environment to aspiring chefs, so the college gives me unique access to this raw pool of talent, who will in time add to the South East culinary experience.

This book encapsulates the varied choice customers have in our counties, from Gastro pubs, Michelin starred restaurants to retailers and cafés, Thackeray's being just one of the exceptional Michelin starred restaurants featured within this book. With three restaurants, we are uniquely placed to understand the changing trends of consumers and understand the wealth of produce available in the region, whether that be demand for Whitstable oysters or succulent lamb from Romney Marsh.

My career has encompassed stays working with the eponymous Marco Pierre White, Roux Brothers and the famous Schrager brand of boutique hotels, each of these experiences has led to the broadening of my skill and knowledge, as a result of which I am delighted to be writing this foreword for you today. Enjoy all the restaurants featured in this lovely book and I look forward to welcoming you to one of mine in the near future.

154
THE ABINGER HATCH

Abinger Lane, Abinger Common, Dorking, RH5 6HZ

01306 730 737
www.theabingerhatch.com Twitter: @theabingerhatch

A beautiful family-run country pub, The Abinger Hatch is an unexpected gem in the rolling countryside of Surrey. Owners Sarah and Andy Powderhill offer a warm welcome to guests by offering a range of exceptional cask ales and high quality food.

Their charming 17th Century venue offers an informal dining experience with a menu created by head chef Stuart Brown. His 15-year-plus experience of Michelin restaurants and London's finest dining rooms has enabled him to create a vibrant and exciting menu.

The Abinger Hatch combines the best features of an archetypal and idyllic country pub with exceptional food.

Andy says: "We are at the heart of the community and everyone is welcome here. Regulars pop in for a drink and a chat, ramblers and cyclists call in for a coffee or something to eat and dinner guests drive from across the region for top quality food."

Sarah adds: "The thing that people love about us is that we're so friendly. People are always welcomed with a smile and a warm hello - and, of course, the food is fantastic."

The Abinger Hatch under promises and over delivers. In the past two years, it has become a word-of-mouth hit among people across the region. And its reputation is spreading further afield.

Cask ales include brews from microbreweries and independents, and the menu features an extensive range of dishes, from light snacks to succulent tender roasts and creative, fine dining options.

Relish Restaurant Rewards
See page 003 for details.

THE
ABINGER
HATCH
FREE HOUSE

"We provide a warm and friendly service and a real sense of belonging," says Andy.
That unique offering is proving to be a recipe for success.

SMOKED SALMON WITH POTATO PANCAKES, WATERCRESS PUREE & HORSERADISH FOAM

SERVES 4

 Burning Sky Plateau Pale Ale
(East Sussex)

Ingredients

400g smoked salmon

Potato Pancakes

250g mashed potato
22ml double cream
32g plain flour
1 egg
1 egg yolk

Watercress Purée

½ banana shallot (finely sliced)
butter (knob of)
1 bunch watercress
salt and pepper (to taste)

Horseradish Sauce (Foam)

½ banana shallot (finely sliced)
butter (knob of)
white wine (splash of)
1 tbsp horseradish cream
500ml double cream

Garnish

baby watercress

Method

For The Potato Pancakes

Add all the ingredients into a bowl and whisk until you have a smooth batter. Place into a piping bag until ready to cook.

Heat a little oil in a non-stick pan. Pipe 3 circles (size of a 20p coin) per person and colour on one side. Flip the pancakes over, then remove the pan from the heat. The residual heat will cook the pancake.

For The Watercress Purée

Lightly fry the shallot in a little butter until soft.

Blanch the watercress in a pan of boiling, salted water (not too long as you want it to keep its bright green colour). Drain any excess water and add to the cooked shallot. Blend until smooth and press through a fine sieve. Allow to cool over a bowl of iced water (this helps to keep the bright green colour).

> **Chef's Tip**
> To get as smooth a purée as possible, press the mix through a fine sieve.

For The Horseradish Sauce (Foam)

Lightly fry the shallot in the butter. When soft, add the white wine and reduce until almost evaporated. Stir in the horseradish and cream and bring to the boil. Once boiled, blend and pass through a fine sieve.

To Assemble

Gently warm the watercress purée and place 3 drops (size of a 10p coin) on each plate. With the top of the spoon, drag away from you making a teardrop shape. Stack 3 pancakes in the centre of each purée drop.

Cut the salmon into 3 strips per person (2½cm x 10cm long). Roll each strip around your finger and turn down the top to resemble a rose shape. Place one of these on each pancake.

Heat the horseradish sauce. Using a stick blender, blitz until you have a froth forming on the top. Use a spoon to remove this and spoon over the top of each salmon rose.

Finish with some baby watercress.

PAN FRIED GNOCCHI WITH BABY SPINACH, SHAVED VEGETABLES, TRUFFLE DRESSING & BREADED EGG

SERVES 4

 Tillingbourne Falls Gold (Golden Ale)
(Surrey)

Ingredients

Gnocchi

2kg floury potatoes (such as Désirée, washed)
200g strong flour
4 egg yolks
10g salt

Truffle Dressing (makes more than required)

1 litre rapeseed oil
45g truffle paste
125ml sherry vinegar
25g salt
2g ground white pepper

Breaded Hen's Egg

4 free-range hen's eggs
white wine vinegar (to add to the water)
1 egg (beaten)
plain flour (to cover)
panko breadcrumbs (to cover)

Shaved Summer Vegetables

4 baby carrots
4 asparagus spears
4 breakfast radishes
(all finely sliced on a *mandolin*)

Salad

500g baby spinach (washed)
Parmesan (for shaving)
pine nuts (toasted)

Method

For The Gnocchi

Preheat the oven to 180°C.

Bake the potatoes for 45 minutes until the flesh is soft. Cut the potatoes in half and scoop out the flesh. Pass through a *mouli* or potato ricer. Weigh 900g of the potato flesh, add the flour, egg yolks and salt. Bring all the ingredients together, but do not knead.

Bring a large pan of salted water to a simmer.

Divide into 3 equal pieces and roll one into a long, sausage shape - about 10p size in diameter. Cut into 2½cm pieces and place on a floured tray.

Pour about 1cm of oil into a deep tray.

Tip the cut gnocchi into the simmering water and wait for them to rise to the surface. Scoop out with a slotted spoon and place in the oiled tray.

Repeat this process with the remaining pieces of gnocchi.

> **Chef's Tip**
> Do not overwork your gnocchi mix. It's not a bread dough so only requires to be brought together, not kneaded.

For The Truffle Dressing

Blitz all the ingredients together until *emulsified*. Store in the fridge in a sterilised jar.

For The Breaded Eggs

Bring a heavy bottomed pan of water to a simmer and add the vinegar (the water should taste of vinegar).

Organise a bowl of iced water. Crack the eggs into ramekins and tip into the simmering water. Cook for 3 minutes, then place directly into the iced water to stop them cooking. Trim the 'tails' off your eggs so they are round.

Dust the eggs in the flour, roll in the beaten egg and finally the breadcrumbs. They will hold their shape better if you leave them resting in the breadcrumbs.

To Assemble

Fry the gnocchi in a non-stick pan, colouring evenly on 2 sides. Lightly salt the shaved vegetables (this helps remove some of the bite). Dress the spinach with the truffle dressing, shave some Parmesan through it and scatter with pine nuts.

Deep fry the breaded eggs (180°C) until golden, about 2 minutes. Place 5 pieces of gnocchi around the outside of 4 large plates. Pile some of the dressed spinach in the centre, add the remaining gnocchi, the spinach and shaved vegetables. Top with the egg.

VANILLA CREME BRULEE WITH SHORTBREAD & STRAWBERRY SHOT

SERVES 8

Hogs Back A over T Barley Wine
(Surrey)

Ingredients

Shortbread
125g butter
38g icing sugar
112g plain flour

Brûlée
700ml double cream
1 vanilla pod
63g sugar
180g egg yolk (approximately 9 egg yolks)
Demerara sugar (to sprinkle)

Strawberry Purée
500g strawberries
caster sugar (to taste)
Bols strawberry liqueur (to taste)

8 ramekin dishes
8 shot glasses

Method

For The Shortbread

Place all the ingredients in a food processor and blend until everything is combined.

Lay out a flat double layer of cling film, about 45cm long.

Place the shortbread mix in a sausage shape and fold the cling film over so both edges meet. Tuck the cling film in and roll it up around the shortbread. Chill for 1 hour.

Preheat the oven to 170°C.

Remove the cling film from the chilled shortbread. Cut into ½cm thick pieces and lay out evenly on a non-stick baking mat (or on buttered greaseproof paper). Bake for 10 minutes.

> **Chef's Tip**
> Don't be afraid to use too much cling film in the shaping of the shortbread.

To Make The Brûlée (Allow 2 hours)

Split the vanilla pod lengthways and put into a heavy bottomed pan with the cream. Bring to the boil, remove from the heat and allow to sit for 5 minutes.

Beat the egg yolk and sugar in a bowl until pale. Pour the cream over the egg mix and whisk in.

Return it to the pan and cook until 84°C on a low heat, whisking continuously.

Pass through a fine sieve and pour into your moulds. Chill for around 1½ hours or until set.

For The Strawberry Purée

Put the strawberries, sugar and a little water into a blender and blitz until smooth. Pass through a fine sieve. Add about half liqueur to two thirds purée (you may prefer a bit more alcohol kick so add more liqueur as you please).

To Assemble

Lightly sprinkle the Demerara sugar over each brûlée and caramelise with a blow torch - do this slowly so as not to burn the sugar. Lightly dust the shortbread with icing sugar. Pour the purée into each shot glass and enjoy.

164
THE FRENCH TABLE

85 Maple Road, Surbiton, Surrey, KT6 4AW

020 8399 2365
www.thefrenchtable.co.uk Twitter: @thefrenchtable Facebook: The French Table

There is a corner of leafy Surrey that is forever à la Française.

The French Table, in verdant Surbiton, thrills to the cuisine of patron chef Eric Guignard and his team.

Eric, and his wife Sarah, are well respected figures in the South East. They opened their gorgeous and stylish restaurant 15 years ago and have never looked back.

French seasonal cooking dominates their sumptuous menus and Eric is in daily contact with his small team of suppliers to source the best ingredients.

Eric is a star act. He learned his trade at Michelin starred restaurants in Paris, cooking at the two star Jacques Cagna and the one star Jules Verne, before decamping to London.

Initially, he planned to remain in England for just two years. "I came here to learn the language," he says. However, his career took off and he was hired at the one star Capital Hotel.

Eric and Sarah opened The French Table the year after the Millennium and serve a discerning clientele.

"The food is seasonal and the menu changes quite a lot," says Eric. "It's all about mood and all about seasons. It's my cooking. I used to have a French style, but it's become more Eric-English-French over the years."

Eric and Sarah own the adjacent French Tarte, a patisserie and boulangerie that serves some of the finest artisan bread, pastry and coffee in the South East. The denizens of Surbiton form an orderly queue for the sort of high quality, authentic food that Eric loved as a boy in south east France.

Relish Restaurant Rewards
See page 003 for details.

PLEASE MIND THE STEP

Vive La France!

SCALLOP & PORK BELLY, CARAMEL & MISO DRESSING, CAULIFLOWER PANNA COTTA, CHORIZO CRUMBLE

SERVES 4

🍷 *Aphros Loureiro, Vinho Verde 2013 (Portugal)*
Refreshing with bright and vibrant acidity.
Pink grapefruit on the nose is complemented with
clean, tropical notes on the finish.

Ingredients

4 large hand-dived scallops

Pork Belly
240g whole pork belly
1 tbsp salt
1 litre vegetable oil
1 tsp peppercorns
1 tsp soy sauce
3 bay leaves
1 shallot
4 cloves garlic
1 star anise
cognac (splash of)
red wine (splash of)
30g honey

Cauliflower Panna Cotta
200g cauliflower
160ml full-fat milk
80ml double cream
4g bronze leaf gelatine (softened in water)
salt (pinch of)
pepper (pinch of)

Chorizo Crumble
80g plain flour
80g unsalted butter
80g chorizo cular rojo (finely diced)

Miso Dressing
200g caster sugar
40ml white wine
200g miso soya bean paste

Garnish
dried olives

4 panna cotta rings (7cm x 3½cm)

Method

For The Pork Belly (Allow 48 hours)

Soak the pork belly in water with the salt for 24 hours.

Preheat the oven to 120°C (fan).

Drain the pork and cook with the vegetable oil, peppercorns, soy sauce, bay leaves, shallot, garlic, star anise, cognac and red wine for 4 hours. Drain and store overnight in the fridge.

Heat the oven to 180°C (fan).

Cube the pork, then caramelise with the honey for 10 minutes.

Chef's Tip

Soak the pork belly with salt for 24 hours for a better flavour.

For The Cauliflower Panna Cotta

Simmer the cauliflower in the milk and cream for 1 hour. Pass the milk through a sieve and stir in the gelatine. Season and pour into rings. Set in the fridge for 1 hour.

For The Chorizo Crumble

Preheat the oven to 180°C (fan).

Mix the flour, butter and chorizo together and bake for 20 minutes until hard.

For The Miso Dressing

Make a caramel with the sugar and white wine. *Deglaze* with a little water when coloured. Stir in the miso paste.

For The Scallops

Cut each scallop in 3, rub with a little oil and blow torch to colour them.

To Serve

Plate the panna cotta, sprinkle with the chorizo crumb and dried olives. Place the scallops with the pork cubes and miso dressing around the panna cotta.

VENISON SADDLE WITH CELERIAC PUREE, GRAPE JELLY, POMMES DAUPHINE, GREEN PEPPERCORN SAUCE

SERVES 4

Faugeres, Clos Fantine, Languedoc-Roussillon, 2012 (France)
Earthy and vivid, lots of terroir notes mixed with plenty of red and black fruits, the mid palate is dense and memorable.

Ingredients

800g venison saddle
olive oil

Grape Jelly

400g black, seedless grapes
1g agar agar

Green Peppercorn Sauce

400g venison bones
50g Spanish onions (diced)
50g carrots (diced), 1 stick celery (diced)
garlic (pinch of)
1g star anise
whole black peppercorns (pinch of)
1g whole cloves, 1 bay leaf
20ml red wine vinegar
1 tbsp 40% cognac
200ml red cooking wine
2 litres veal stock
8g green peppercorns, butter (knob of)

Celeriac Purée

240g celeriac (cut into large dice)
80g unsalted butter
100ml double cream
salt (pinch of)

Pommes Dauphine

200g red potatoes
150ml water, 80g unsalted butter
salt (pinch of)
120g plain flour
3 medium organic eggs

Garnish

4 black seedless grapes (cut into quarters)

Method

For The Grape Jelly (Prepare ahead)

Blitz the grapes in a blender. Bring to the boil and add the agar agar. Pass through a sieve and leave to set in the fridge for 3 hours. Once set, cut into cubes.

For The Green Peppercorn Sauce

Colour the venison bones with the onions, carrots, celery and garlic (*mirepoix*), bay leaf and spices. *Deglaze* the pan with the red wine vinegar and reduce until dry. *Deglaze* with the cognac and red wine, then add the stock. Cook for 2 hours, then pass through a sieve and chill. Reduce to a sauce consistency, add the green peppercorns and finish with butter.

For The Celeriac Purée

Preheat the oven to 180°C (fan).

Wrap the celeriac in foil with the butter and bake for 40 minutes until soft. Blend with the cream and season with salt.

For The Pommes Dauphine

Preheat the oven to 180°C (fan).

Bake the potatoes for 45 minutes until soft, discard the skins and mash the flesh.

Boil the water with the butter and salt. Add the flour and incorporate the eggs, one by one, until smooth. Stir into the mashed potato.

Roll the mix to form about 20 balls. Deep fry at 180°C for 20 seconds until golden.

For The Venison Saddle

Preheat the oven to 180°C (fan).

Pan fry the saddle of venison in a hot pan with the oil to seal it, then place in the oven for 6 minutes. Remove from the oven and leave to rest for 5 minutes.

To Serve

Assemble as pictured.

GINGERBREAD & BUTTER PUDDING WITH POACHED PEAR

SERVES 4

 *Classic Pedro Ximenez Fernando De Castilla (Spain)
Made from sun-dried grapes, this seductive, sweet
wine has a thick, silky, syrupy texture with luscious
grape, raisin and prune flavours.*

Ingredients

Gingerbread

360g black treacle
360g golden syrup
160g soft dark brown sugar
280g Pamplie butter
720g wholemeal flour
0.8g table salt
16g gluten free baking powder
16g ground ginger
24g Chinese 5 spice
160ml pasteurised whole egg
240ml full-fat milk

Butter Pudding

256ml whole pasteurised egg
80ml pasteurised egg yolk
1 tsp sugar
160ml whipping cream
50 unsalted butter

Milk Ice Cream

600ml full-fat milk
1 bronze gelatine leaf (soaked)
250g condensed milk
100g Suprema milk powder
75ml double cream
125g caster sugar

Milk Purée

450ml full-fat milk
45g caster sugar
1 vanilla pod
4½g agar agar

To Serve

4 poached pears

20cm x 20cm cake tin (greased)

Method

For The Gingerbread (Must be made a day in advance)

Preheat the oven to 200°C (fan).

Boil the treacle, syrup, brown sugar and butter together. Sift the flour, salt, baking powder and spices and pour into the melted ingredients, beating with a flat spoon.

Whisk together the egg and milk, then beat this, bit by bit, into the mix. Pour into the prepared cake tin. Place in the oven and turn the heat down to 180°C (fan). Bake for 10 minutes, then turn the oven to 160°C (fan) and bake for 20 minutes. Check that a knife inserted comes out clear to ensure it is baked through.

For The Butter Pudding

Preheat the oven to 140°C (fan).

The next day, slice the gingerbread into 1cm thick pieces. Line a tray with parchment paper and neatly lay in the slices, overlapping each other.

Whisk the yolk, whole eggs and sugar together. Boil the cream and pour over the eggs, whisking constantly. Pour this over the sliced gingerbread and leave for 20 minutes to absorb the custard. Bake for 25 minutes until the custard is softly set, like a crème brûlée. Cool, then slice into portions.

For The Milk Ice Cream

Reduce the milk by half, then stir in the gelatine. Mix the condensed milk with the milk powder and cream, then pour in the reduced milk and the sugar, stirring until the sugar dissolves. Transfer to a container and freeze until set.

For The Milk Purée

Bring the milk, caster sugar, vanilla pod and agar agar to the boil, then remove from the heat.

Pour into a container and set in the fridge - about 3 hours. Blitz in a blender to make into a purée.

To Serve

Preheat the oven to 180°C (fan).

Flash the gingerbread in the oven for 5 minutes to warm. Sprinkle some caster sugar on the top and caramelise using a blow torch (like crème brûlée). Serve with poached pear.

174
THE MINNIS
BAR & RESTAURANT

The Parade, Minnis Bay, Birchington, Kent, CT7 9QP

01843 841 844
www.theminnis.co.uk Twitter: @theminnis Facebook: The Minnis Restaurant

f modern gastronomy can sometimes be guilty of being all style over substance, The Minnis is an exception. The 'end of the road', seaside bar and restaurant has a simple philosophy: flavour is king.

Its French-English menu delivers time after time by putting the tastebuds of its customers first. Don't be deceived however, into thinking The Minnis is undeserving of its place among the South East's big guns.

Jason Freedman's venue has hidden depths. Its bacon, for instance, is cured on the premises while its butter is smoked in an on-site smokery. The tender, succulent fish that attracts so many of its customers is hauled from seas within eyesight of the dining room. Food quite literally does not get any fresher.

Freedman spent many years working in fine dining restaurants before having his 'eureka' moment. "Diners love to eat things that taste great," he says. "It really is that simple. People love great taste and that's what we deliver."

Freedman and his right hand man, Kevin Faux, run one of the South East's busiest venues. During high summer, day-trippers from across the region beat a path for lunch and dinner. The Minnis has queues outside the door as people make a beeline for their home from home.

Freedman adds: "We have a wonderful team here. Kevin and I are ably supported by great chefs and a friendly and engaging front of house team."

So is The Minnis all about passion rather than pretence; about authenticity rather than artifice; about simplicity rather than smoke and mirrors? Kevin smiles and says: "No, it's just about great flavour."

Relish Restaurant Rewards
See page 003 for details.

One of the things which makes The Minnis so special is that they cure, pickle, brine, salt and smoke their own produce on site. It has become known as the place to go to find first class, full flavoured dishes with a difference.

HOME SMOKED LOCAL WOOD PIGEON, BLACK PUDDING, ENGLISH WATERCRESS, SPICED APPLE & APPLE PUREE

SERVES 4

Niel Joubert, Oak Aged Pinotage 2011
(South Africa)

Ingredients

Pigeon

8 cold smoked wood pigeon breasts
8 slices good black pudding
butter (knob of)
freshly ground salt and pepper

The Sauce

1 litre veal stock (*jus lié*)

Apple Purée

1 Kentish green apple (peeled, cored)
1 tbsp cider vinegar
butter (knob of)

Spiced Apple

1 Kentish green apple (peeled, cored)
1 tsp mixed spice (coriander, cinnamon, nutmeg, caraway, allspice, cloves, cardamom, ginger)
butter (knob of)

Garnish

1 bunch English watercress

Method

For The Pigeon

Place a sauté pan over a medium heat, melt a little butter and add the slices of black pudding. Cook for 1 minute each side, remove and keep warm. Increase the heat and place the pigeon breasts in the same pan. Season with salt and pepper and cook for 1 minute until brown. Add a small amount of butter, turn and cook for a further 1½-2 minutes, basting the pigeon constantly with the hot, melted butter (the breasts should be rare). Remove and let the pigeon rest somewhere warm.

For The Sauce

Reduce the stock to around 250ml to create a sauce.

For The Apple Purée

Chop the apple finely and place in a pan with the cider vinegar and a little butter. Cook until soft, purée in a blender or by hand, and pass through a sieve to make a smooth purée. Season with salt and pepper.

For The Spiced Apple

Cut the apple into 12 small wedges. Melt a little butter in a pan, add the spices and cook gently to release their natural oils and flavours. Add the apple wedges and cook until golden, but still firm.

To Assemble

Slice the pigeon breasts in half and arrange on 4 warm plates with the slices of black pudding and the spiced apple. Lay on a few stalks and leaves of watercress, pour over a little of the reduced veal stock, then dot the apple purée around the plate.

Chef's Tip

We make our own black pudding and smoke our pigeon in-house. Your local butcher should be able to help with these. Use cold smoked pigeon as it is going to be cooked. This dish reflects perfectly everything great about a lovely, autumn day.

JACOB'S LADDER OF KENTISH BEEF, BOURGUIGNON SAUCE, SMOKED MASH, HORSERADISH & PARSNIP PUREE

SERVES 4

 Fleurie AC CRU Beaujolais 2011
(France)

Ingredients

Jacob's Ladder

4 x Jacob's ladder (short ribs) of Kentish beef
(ask your butcher to prepare the ribs for you)
rosemary and thyme (a few sprigs of)
freshly ground salt and pepper
100ml olive oil

Bourguignon Sauce

200ml good red wine
200g smoked bacon lardons (pancetta)
20 baby onions (peeled)
20 small chestnut mushrooms
1 tbsp fresh parsley (chopped)
2 tsp tomato purée
500ml rich beef stock

Smoked Mash

1kg floury white potatoes (peeled, diced)
250g smoked butter
200ml double cream
freshly ground salt and pepper

Horseradish And Parsnip Purée

250g fresh horseradish (grated)
250g parsnip (grated)
400ml milk
freshly ground salt and pepper

Garnish

2 carrots and 1 small swede
(Both peeled and cut to desired shape - cook in
salted water, drain, then season and toss in a
little butter)

Chef's Tip

We smoke our own butter but you can use powdered
or liquid smoke to enhance the mashed potato.

Method

For The Jacob's Ladder (Prepare the day before)
Pour the oil into a bowl and add the salt, pepper, fresh thyme
and rosemary. Mix well, adding a little force to bring out the
natural oils in the herbs. Add the ribs to the bowl and coat well.
Cover and leave overnight.
Preheat the oven to 170°C.
Heat a heavy bottomed pan over a high heat, add the ribs and
cook for a few minutes on each side until beautifully brown and
caramelised. Remove the ribs from the pan and place into a
casserole dish. Cook in the oven for 45 minutes.
Meanwhile, add the red wine to the juices and herbs in the pan
and reduce by half. Pour into a bowl and set aside.

For The Bourguignon Sauce
Place the pan back on a high heat. Add the lardons, onions,
mushrooms and parsley and brown them nicely. Stir in the
tomato purée and the reserved red wine cooking juices.
Cook until the liquid has almost evaporated. Add the rich beef
stock and reduce by half.
Pour the sauce over the beef and return to the oven to cook
for a further 4 hours until tender (the meat will shrink back
along the bone).

For The Smoked Mash
Cook the potatoes in boiling, salted water until soft. Drain and
return to the pan. Dry the potatoes out as much as possible by
stirring them over a low heat. Using a masher or potato ricer,
mash the potatoes, season with salt and pepper, then add the
smoked butter and double cream. Beat the potatoes vigorously
until they are smooth and creamy (do not use a food processor
or mixer, or they will release their starch and go like glue).

For The Horseradish And Parsnip Purée
Place all the ingredients into a pan and bring to the boil. Cook
until soft then drain, reserving the milk. Purée the vegetable by
hand or in a blender until smooth (add a little of the reserved
milk if required). Taste and adjust seasoning accordingly.

To Assemble
Place the smoked mash on 4 warmed plates and lay a Jacob's
ladder on top. Add the horseradish and parsnip purée, then the
carrot and swede. Pour over the sauce allowing 5 onions and
5 mushrooms per plate and of course some lovely, smoked
bacon. Grab 4 knives and forks, 3 friends, tuck in and enjoy!
Flavour is king.

THE BEST CHOCOLATE TART EVER! DRINKING CHOCOLATE ICE CREAM, BRITTLE & RASPBERRY COULIS

SERVES 8

 Kleindal Muscat Colombard 2013 (South Africa)

Ingredients

Pastry

90g plain flour (plus a little more for dusting)
40g icing sugar
20g good quality 70% cocoa powder
70g butter
1 egg yolk

Chocolate Ganache

130ml double cream
45g good dark chocolate (see chef's tip)
50ml Tia Maria (optional)

Drinking Chocolate Ice Cream

3 egg yolks
250g sugar
450ml double cream
200g drinking chocolate powder
100g dark chocolate (grated)

Brittle

100gm caster sugar
50g hazelnuts or peanuts (toasted)
1 tbsp water
lemon juice (drop of)

Raspberry Coulis

250g fresh raspberries
1 tbsp icing sugar
(Gently heat the ingredients until the raspberries bleed. Blend until smooth, then pass through a fine sieve)

Garnish

biscuit crumbs, chocolate straws, physalis

18cm x 6cm loose bottomed baking tray (lightly buttered)

Method

For The Pastry

Sift the dry ingredients into a large bowl. Bind the butter into the flour mix using your fingers to form a crumb. Add the yolk and mix to a paste, adding a few drops of cold water if required. Wrap in cling film and rest in the fridge for 2 hours until firm. Unwrap the pastry and roll out on a lightly floured surface to 0.5cm thick.
Line the tin with the pastry and blind bake for 25 minutes at 170°C (fan). Remove the baking beans and return to the oven for 10 minutes to crisp up the pastry. Remove from the oven, leave to cool, then trim off any excess pastry.

For The Chocolate Ganache

Bring the cream to the boil in a saucepan. Remove from the heat at once and stir in the Tia Maria (if using) and chocolate until it has melted to create an amazing, rich, chocolate sauce. Pour into the tart case and allow to cool for 1 hour before placing in the fridge.

For The Drinking Chocolate Ice Cream

In a *bain-marie*, add the yolks and sugar. Heat gently whilst continuously whisking until pale and light. Bring the cream to the boil in a pan, then remove from the heat. Add the chocolate and powder, and whisk until melted and smooth.
Allow to cool slightly. Add the chocolate cream mix to the eggs and heat very gently (if it is too hot, the eggs will scramble) whisking continuously until the mix leaves ribbons behind.
Allow to cool, then churn in an ice cream machine. Store in the freezer.

For The Brittle

Place the sugar, water and lemon juice in a heavy bottomed pan. Cook to a light caramel, swirling the pan gently from time to time but do not stir as it will crystalise. When golden, add the nuts. Working quickly, pour the mix onto a baking sheet lined with silicon paper. Let it cool completely.

To Assemble

Serve as pictured. This is the most delicious chocolate tart in the world and you will want more... guaranteed!

> **Chef's Tip**
> Use the best quality chocolate that you can buy and make sure it's at least 70% cocoa. Take your time over the pastry.

184
READ'S
RESTAURANT WITH ROOMS

Macknade Manor, Canterbury Road, Faversham, Kent, ME13 8XE

01795 535 344
www.reads.com

For almost four decades Rona and David Pitchford have been offering refined, elegant food with particular fine service. Set in an elegant Georgian manor house, Read's Restaurant with Rooms is located on the outskirts of Faversham, surrounded by tranquil grounds, with lawns shaded by lofty cedar, weeping willow and horse chestnut trees.

The food has always preserved a proud British element with the use of vegetables and fruit from the kitchen garden, alongside the well chosen local suppliers of the Kent countryside and coast. An extensive wine list balances the French classics with a carefully chosen and imaginative selection from Europe, the Americas and the New World, along with a comprehensive selection of half bottles and a condensed list of 'Best Buys'.

Read's also offers six restful and relaxed guest bedrooms, each one individually designed and furnished in period style, with traditional English fabrics and all of them with modern, en suite bathrooms.

Its location, close to Canterbury, means that Read's is perfectly placed for anyone in search of somewhere rather exceptional to stay. The surrounding Kentish countryside is the perfect location for country walks or bird watching at the Oare marshes. Best of all, a short break here offers a rare opportunity to enjoy the very essence of English country living.

Relish Restaurant Rewards
See page 003 for details.

With 21 consecutive years of holding a Michelin star and
the top ten South East Restaurants in the Hardens Guide
100 UK Restaurants, Read's widespread reputation is
founded on the distinctive cooking of David Pitchford,
whose seasonal dishes blend herbs and vegetables from
the manor's own walled, kitchen garden.

MACKEREL RILLETTE WITH COX APPLE JELLY, PICKLED CARROTS & CUCUMBER SALAD

SERVES 4

 Sybille Kuntz Riesling 2010
(Germany)

Ingredients

Mackerel Rillette

4 fillets cold smoked mackerel
10g dill pickles (chopped)
½ shallot (finely chopped)
½ lemon (juice of)
1 tbsp mayonnaise
1 tbsp crème fraîche
5g parsley (chopped)
1 tsp horseradish

Apple Jelly

500ml Cox's apple juice
2 leaves gelatine (soaked in cold water)

Pickled Carrots

1 carrot (peeled)
60ml white wine vinegar
40g sugar
½ star anise
3 peppercorns
½ shallot (sliced)
1 bay leaf

Cucumber And Apple Salad

1 cucumber (peeled)
½ apple (peeled)

Garnish

chervil
toasted flutes (thinly sliced bread drizzled with
olive oil and gently baked until crisp)

4 x 5cm tall by 5cm diameter rings

Method

For The Mackerel Rillette (Prepare at least 6 hours before)

Grill the mackerel fillets for 6 minutes, then leave to cool.
Remove the skin and the blood line with a spoon. Flake the
mackerel into a mixing bowl.

Add the dill pickles, shallot, lemon juice, mayonnaise,
crème fraîche, parsley and horseradish, then mix together.
Taste and season.

Spoon the mixture into rings, pressing firmly down. Make sure
you leave a little space for the jelly to sit on top of the mixture.

Leave to cool in the fridge for 4-6 hours.

For The Apple Jelly

Bring the apple juice to the boil and reduce by half. Stir in the
soaked gelatine until dissolved.

Allow to cool, then pour on the top of the mackerel mixture.
Leave to set for 10-15 minutes.

For The Pickled Carrots

Cut the carrot into long, thin matchstick strips (*julienne*).

Mix all the ingredients for the pickling *liquor* together and bring
to the boil in a saucepan.

Transfer to a bowl and add the carrots.

> **Chef's Tip**
> Keep the carrots in the pickling *liquor* for as long as possible
> to enhance the flavour.

For The Cucumber And Apple Salad

Finely slice the cucumber into discs. Cut the raw apple into
small dice.

To Plate

Place a ring of the thinly sliced cucumber on the centre of the
plate overlapping as you go.

Gently help the mackerel mixture from the mould and place in
the centre of the cucumber ring. Take 5 cubes of the apple and
arrange them evenly around the edge of the cucumber.

Place a piece of the pickled carrot over the top of the apple.
Garnish with chervil and drizzle with a little olive oil to finish
(if desired) and serve.

A CELEBRATION OF KENTISH LAMB

SERVES 4

 Viña Arana Reserve 2005
(Spain)

Ingredients

Loin Of Lamb On Buttered Baby Spinach

1 boned-out loin of lamb
1 shallot (finely chopped)
1 clove garlic (finely chopped)
1 tbsp extra virgin olive oil
250g baby spinach leaves
25g unsalted butter, seasoning

Rack Of Lamb On Sweetheart Cabbage

1 rack of lamb (with 4 cutlets, seasoned)
1 small sweetheart cabbage (finely shredded)
20g butter, 20ml olive oil

Lamb's Kidney And Fondant Potato

2 lamb's kidneys
4 small potatoes (peeled, shaped)
475ml chicken stock
20g butter, 20ml olive oil
4 sprigs rosemary, seasoning

Individual Shepherd's Pies

200g braising lamb (rump would be good)
½ litre chicken stock
1 carrot (finely diced)
1 small onion (finely diced)
450g potatoes (peeled, washed)
20g butter (melted)
1 egg
30ml double cream

Carrot Purée

2-3 good size carrots (peeled, cut into small dice)
1 shallot (peeled, finely sliced)
1 clove garlic (puréed)
300ml double cream

Rosemary Jus

1 litre lamb stock (reduced by two thirds)
2 glasses red wine (Cabernet Sauvignon)
handful fresh rosemary leaves, seasoning

4 individual small pie dishes

Method

For The Loin Of Lamb On Buttered Baby Spinach

Season and pan fry the loin in olive oil, then rest. Sweat the shallot and garlic in butter, add the spinach, then wilt. Drain and season. Spoon the spinach onto 4 serving plates, slice the lamb and arrange on top.

Rack Of Lamb On Sweetheart Cabbage

Preheat the oven to 180°C.

Seal the rack in hot olive oil, roast in the oven for 7-8 minutes (to serve pink) and rest.

Cook the cabbage in a very small amount of water until just cooked. Drain, season and butter.

Cut into 4 cutlets and place each one on the top of a spoonful of cabbage.

Lamb's Kidney And Fondant Potato

Slice the kidneys lengthways and remove the outside membrane. Remove the white gristle part from the centre. Season and cook the kidneys in olive oil for 1-2 minutes each side.

Simmer the potatoes in the chicken stock and butter until tender. Plate with the kidney on top and garnish with rosemary.

Individual Shepherd's Pies

Gently poach the lamb in the stock for 1 hour until tender. Remove and dice. Reduce the stock by half.

Simmer the potatoes in salted, boiling water until tender. Mash, then finish with the cream, butter and egg yolk.

Sauté the vegetables in butter until soft. Combine with the stock and diced lamb. Spoon into 4 pie dishes. Pipe the potato on top and glaze under a grill.

> #### Chef's Tip
>
> Use diced rump of lamb for the braising meat in the shepherd's pie for a tasty alternative to mince.

For The Carrot Purée

Sauté the shallot and garlic until soft. Add the carrot and cook gently for 10 minutes. Add the cream and simmer for 5 minutes. Blitz in a blender, then pass through a fine sieve.

For The Rosemary Jus

Combine the reduced lamb stock and wine, then reduce again by half. *Deglaze* the lamb cooking pans with this stock. Add any meat juices from the resting meat. Gently bring to a simmer, add the rosemary and cook for 5 minutes. Pass through a fine strainer. Season to taste.

To Serve

Assemble the dish as in the photograph.

MIXED BERRY SOUFFLE

SERVES 4

🍷 *Edmeades Late Harvest Zinfandel 2006*
(California, USA)

Ingredients

Base Mixture

250g mixed berries
85g sugar
11g cornflour
2 tbsp water

Soufflé

40g caster sugar
90g egg white (3-4 medium eggs)
150g mixed berry base mixture

To Serve

vanilla ice cream
4 shortbread biscuits

4 ramekins (greased with 5g soft butter and
2 tbsp caster sugar for coating)

Method

For The Base Mixture

Add the mixed berries and 25g of sugar to a pan. Cook until a thick purée is produced.

Whilst the berries are cooking, mix the cornflour with the water to form a paste, then set aside.

Blitz the berry mixture in a blender until smooth, then pass through a fine sieve.

Return the mixture to the heat and add the remaining sugar. Bring to the boil.

Reduce the heat to a simmer, add the cornflour mixture and cook for a further 2 minutes.

Pass the mixture through a fine sieve again and set aside in a large mixing bowl for later.

For The Soufflé

Whisk the egg whites until firm peaks form, then add the sugar and continue to whisk until it reaches a firm peak.

Take a third of the meringue mixture and beat into the mixed berry base mix.

Once mixed together, add the remaining meringue mix and gently fold into the berry mix. Set aside in the fridge.

When You Are Ready To Serve

Preheat the oven to 180°C (fan).

Brush the ramekins with the soft butter to form a light, even coating on the inside of each dish. Pour the sugar into the first ramekin. Hold over the second ramekin and turn slowly so the entire inside is coated with the sugar. Once complete, pour the excess sugar into the second ramekin and repeat until all 4 ramekins are buttered and sugared.

Transfer the soufflé mix into a piping bag and pipe to the top of each ramekin. Use a palette knife to smooth over, keeping the mixture flush to the rim of the ramekin. Ease the mixture away from the edge of the ramekin with the tip of a knife.

Place the ramekins on a baking tray and bake the soufflés in the oven for 7-9 minutes.

Remove from the oven and serve immediately with vanilla ice cream and shortbread.

Chef's Tip

When brushing the ramekins with butter, work in upward strokes to help encourage the soufflé to rise evenly.

194
THE SWAN

35 Swan Street, West Malling, Kent, ME19 6JU

01732 521 910
www.theswanwestmalling.co.uk Twitter: @swanwm

Located in the picturesque Kentish market town of West Malling, The Swan, once a 15th Century inn, is a firm favourite. The stunning restaurant, awarded two AA Rosettes and is Michelin recommended, has a beautiful, cocktail bar situated on the ground floor. Upstairs there is a sophisticated, private lounge bar and three other unique private rooms, perfectly suited for dining and social gatherings.

In warmer months, the beautiful garden is open for diners, drinkers, events and gatherings. The peaceful top terrace is the perfect wedding venue in the summer months.

The style of food is modern British. Co-owner Darryl Healy and head chef Lee Edney offer a menu inspired by local, seasonal produce with venison, pork and lamb, all purchased from local farms, providing 100% provenance to customers. During the game season, wild shot pheasant and mallard are regular menu staples, supplied by Kentfield Farm in Offham, one of the neighbouring villages. "We work closely with the producers," says Lee. "We have great relationships. They tell us what's available and it goes straight on the menu."

All dishes are prepared with skill and integrity so that the produce is always the main focus. Signature dishes include 'King scallops, chorizo crumb and Calvados apples'; 'Rib of beef for two with gratin dauphinoise and cep ragout'; 'Gypsy tart with peanut butter ice cream and honeycomb'.

The wine list offers superb quality as well as value, with a blend of boutique and lesser known producers, through to some great classics from the old world. The wine dinners are renowned in the area and are hosted by Nick Levantis, Darryl's fellow co-owner and the charismatic sommelier, Vincent Gasnier.

Relish Restaurant Rewards
See page 003 for details.

"Our aim at The Swan has always been to create a restaurant that everyone would love to have around the corner; neighbourhood and customer focused, with a fantastic atmosphere, robust food, a great wine list, offering relaxed yet professional service. A restaurant that all staff feel proud to be a part of and one that all customers look forward to returning to time and time again!" Darryl Healy.

SALMON GRAVLAX, CITRUS, CUCUMBER & WASABI EMULSION

SERVES 4

*Sancerre, Terres Blanches 2012, Domain Thomas
(Loire, France)*

Ingredients

Salmon

600g salmon fillet
300g salt
90g sugar
5g coriander seeds (crushed)
5g white peppercorns (crushed)
2 lemons (zest and juice of)
1 orange (zest and juice of)
1 stick lemongrass (crushed)

To Finish The Cured Salmon

50g dill (finely chopped)
1 tbsp Dijon mustard

Lemon Gel

100ml water
100g sugar
3g agar agar
2 lemons

Wasabi Emulsion

20g wasabi powder
10ml water
25g pasteurised egg yolk (1-2 eggs)
25ml olive oil
50ml vegetable oil
2ml white wine vinegar
5ml lemon juice
1g table salt

Garnish

cucumber flowers
cucumber dice
apple batons
coriander cress
sliced radish
burnt butter powder

Method

For The Salmon Gravlax (Prepare 24 Hours Before)

Mix together the salt, sugar, coriander seeds, peppercorn seeds, lemon zest, orange zest and lemongrass and sprinkle heavily all over the salmon fillet (both sides). Wrap in cling film and leave for 12 hours to cure. After 12 hours, gently rinse the cure from the salmon and dry on a j-cloth. Lightly spread the Dijon mustard on top of the salmon and sprinkle the chopped dill to cover the mustard. Wrap tightly in cling film and refrigerate.

For The Lemon Gel

Zest one of the lemons, remove the pith and cut the flesh into quarters. Bring the sugar, water, lemon zest and quarters to the boil. Pass through a sieve and bring back to the boil. Add the agar agar and use a blender to mix together thoroughly. Boil for a further 2 minutes to ensure the agar agar has cooked. Set in a tray. When set, blitz in a blender with the juice of the remaining lemon to bring it together to form a gel. Adjust the consistency with a splash of water if the gel is too thick.

For The Wasabi Emulsion

Mix the wasabi powder with the water to form a paste. Whisk in the egg yolk and vinegar and combine well. Slowly add both oils to the wasabi mixture whilst whisking to form the *emulsion*. Season with lemon juice and salt to taste.

To Serve

Portion the salmon into 12 cubes, remove the blood line and serve 3 pieces to each guest. Evenly use the lemon gel and wasabi *emulsion* to garnish the plate and assemble the other garnishes as desired.

Chef's Tip

You can prepare all the elements for this dish 1 or 2 days in advance. Assemble just before serving.

RIB OF BEEF TO SHARE, CEPS, POTATO DAUPHINOISE, ROASTED BONE MARROW

SERVES 4

🍷 *Vino Nobile di Montepulciano 2010, Braccesca (Tuscany, Italy)*

Ingredients

2 x 900g rib eye steaks on the bone (seasoned with sea salt, black pepper and a drizzle of olive oil)

Potato Dauphinoise

1kg Désirée potatoes (peeled and sliced thinly on a *mandolin*)
olive oil (to drizzle)
400ml double cream
1 bay leaf
1 garlic clove (peeled, crushed)
200g medium Cheddar cheese (grated)
sea salt and freshly ground black pepper

Bone Marrow

2 x 12cm bone marrow (split lengthways, scored and seasoned)
100g breadcrumbs
20g thyme
20g flat leaf parsley
5g rosemary
3g grated horseradish

Bordelaise Sauce

500ml Bordeaux red wine
3 banana shallots (finely diced)
500ml beef stock
30g bone marrow (finely diced)

To Serve

200g ceps (4 large ceps if possible)
olive oil
butter (knob of)

Method

For The Beef

Preheat the oven to 210°C.

Sear the seasoned rib eye for 4 minutes on each side on a heated chargrill (or grill pan), then transfer to the oven for 10-12 minutes. Remove from the oven and rest on a cooling rack for 15 minutes.

> **Chef's Tip**
>
> Try to source dry aged beef that is well-marbled. Once cooked, allow to rest for a minimum of 15 minutes before serving.

For The Potato Dauphinoise

Preheat the oven to 160°C.

Lightly oil a large deep ceramic baking dish, or 4 individual dishes. Put the cream, bay leaf and garlic in a pan and heat until simmering. When the liquid begins to bubble up the sides of the pan, turn off the heat and leave to cool slightly.

Scatter a third of the cheese over the bottom of the dish and cover with a layer of potato slices, overlapping slightly. Season with salt and pepper. Continue layering until you've used all the cheese and potatoes, seasoning the layers and finishing with cheese. Strain the cream, discarding the bay leaf and garlic. Pour over the potatoes to come two thirds up the sides. Gently press the potatoes down to help absorb the liquid. Sprinkle with more cheese and bake for 45-60 minutes, or until the potatoes are golden brown and tender when prodded with a sharp knife. Leave to stand for a few minutes before serving.

For The Bordelaise Sauce

Add the shallots to the wine, bring to the boil and reduce by half. Add the beef stock, bring back to the boil, then allow to reduce on a low heat until the sauce coats the back of a spoon. Add the finely diced bone marrow just before serving. This helps to enrich the sauce.

For The Bone Marrow

Preheat the oven to 180°C.

Bake the bone marrow in the oven for 8 minutes. Blitz the breadcrumbs with the herbs and sprinkle over the top of the bone marrow. Bake for a further 2 minutes.

To Serve

Cut the ceps in half and criss cross score the flesh side. Pan fry for 4 minutes in a little olive oil and butter. Carve the beef and assemble garnishes as pictured.

TOASTED MARSHMALLOW, CHOCOLATE, ALMOND BRITTLE, PEANUT BUTTER ICE CREAM

SERVES 4

🍷 *Moscato, Maculan, Dindarello, 2012*
(Veneto, Italy)

Ingredients

Marshmallow

120g egg white (from 3-4 eggs)
455g caster sugar
1 vanilla pod (split lengthways, scraped)
200ml water
50g glucose
4 bronze gelatine leaves (soaked)
50g cornflour
50g icing sugar

Peanut Butter Ice Cream

100g caster sugar
100g egg yolk (from 5-6 eggs)
250ml double cream
250ml full-fat milk
50g peanut butter

Chocolate Paint

50g cocoa butter
50g dark chocolate

Almond Brittle

100g flaked almonds (toasted)
100g caster sugar
50g butter
50ml water

Garnish

raspberry purée
pistachios (crushed)
redcurrants

Method

For The Marshmallow

Whisk the egg whites to a soft peak.

Boil the sugar, water, vanilla pod and glucose over a moderate heat to 121°C. Remove from the heat and extract the vanilla pod with tongs as it will be extremely hot. Squeeze the excess water from the gelatine, add to the hot liquid and allow to melt.

Slowly add the sugar mixture to the whisking soft peak egg whites. Once all the sugar has been incorporated, continue to whisk until the mixture begins to cool down. Transfer the '*Italian meringue*' mixture to a container lined with cling film and dusted with some of the icing sugar and cornflour. Once cool and firm, turn out and portion into rectangles, dusting again with the icing sugar and cornflour mix.

For The Peanut Butter Ice Cream

Place the milk and cream into a heavy bottomed pan and bring to the boil. Remove from the heat. Whisk the egg yolks and sugar together in a bowl until pale and fluffy, then slowly whisk in the milk and cream mixture until well combined. Return the custard to a clean pan and cook over a medium - low heat for 5-6 minutes, until it thickens enough to coat the back of a wooden spoon. Whisk in the peanut butter and set aside to cool completely. Pour the custard mixture into an ice cream machine and churn. Spoon into a freezer-proof plastic container and chill in the freezer until ready to serve. Remove from the freezer 5 minutes before serving to soften.

For The Chocolate Paint

Melt the cocoa butter and chocolate together over a *bain-marie* and leave in a warm place to keep melted.

For The Almond Brittle

Boil the sugar, butter and water until a toffee caramel colour, pour over the toasted almonds, then allow to cool and set. Carefully break the brittle to get shards of almonds.

To Serve

Brush the chocolate paint across the plate, providing an area to build the dessert on. Blow torch the marshmallow lightly to get a toasted effect and flavour. Assemble the other garnishes over and around the marshmallow for a playful presentation.

204
THACKERAY'S RESTAURANT

85 London Road, Tunbridge Wells, Kent, TN1 1EA

01892 511 921
www.thackerays-restaurant.co.uk Twitter: @ThackeraysRest Facebook: Thackeray's

T he author of Vanity Fair lent his name to Thackeray's restaurant, in leafy Tunbridge Wells. William Thackeray stayed at the shingle-fronted property during the mid-19th Century, a period of intense creativity for one of Britain's greatest writers.

Were Thackeray staying in the restaurant today, he might well be moved to wax lyrical about the starry cuisine from head chef Shane Hughes.

Hughes previously won a Michelin star at the beautiful Relais & Chateaux Hotel Ynyshir Hall in Wales, and his intuitive understanding of classical French cuisine is eye-opening. His superlative food is combined with memorable service at Thackeray's to create an enchanting experience for diners.

Thackeray's is one of the UK's finest restaurants and is a multiple award-winner. Its cuisine delights visitors from around the country, having held three AA Rosettes for 14 consecutive years and being awarded a Michelin star in the first year of it opening, and again for the last three years. The Good Food Guide awarded a score of six, rejoicing in the balance and depth of flavour in dishes and the use of quality ingredients.

Not that Hughes and his team are content. They are keen that the Grade II Listed venue ascends to a higher level and becomes recognised as one of the UK's absolute best. "We're looking to move up a gear. There's a terrific amount of work going on to take us higher, " says Hughes.

Thackeray's diners can enjoy eating in sophisticatedly furnished, themed rooms, including an African room and a fish room. William Thackeray would doubtless be moved to purple prose were he to see the excellence created in the 21st Century restaurant bearing his name.

Relish Restaurant Rewards
See page 003 for details.

Hughes' superlative food is combined with memorable service at Thackeray's to create an enchanting experience for diners.

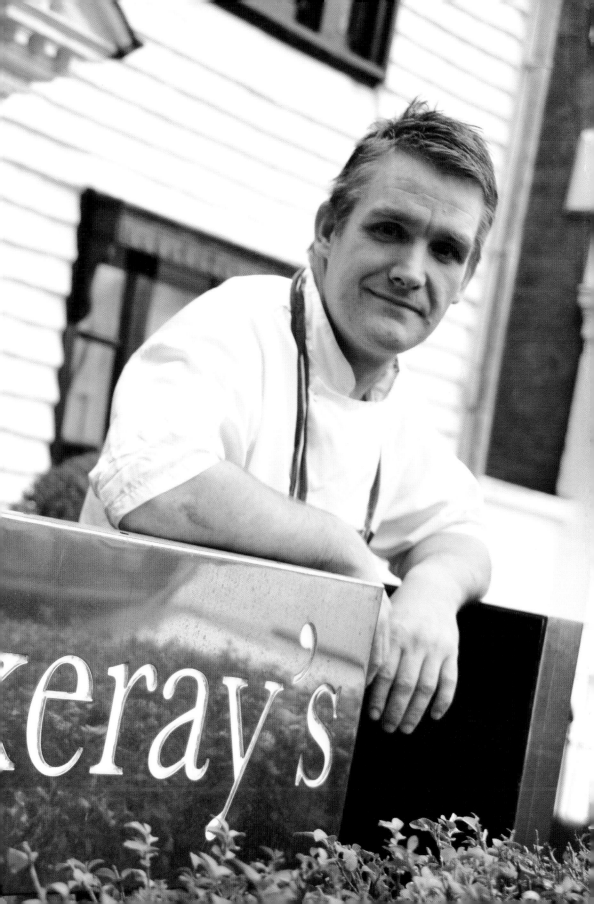

SLOW COOKED KENTISH RABBIT WITH ORKNEY SCALLOPS, MOZZARELLA, TARRAGON PUREE, SWEET & SOUR MUSTARD DRESSING, RABBIT JELLY

SERVES 4

 Pinot Gris, Grand Cru, Sonnenglanz, Domaine Bott-Geyl (France)

Ingredients

2 rabbits (wild is better, innards and head removed)

Sweet And Sour Mustard Dressing

600ml white vinegar
15g red chillies
250g sugar
50g fresh horseradish (grated)
1 sprig thyme, 1 bay leaf
18g cornflour, 15g turmeric
75g Dijon mustard

Tarragon Purée

3 bunches tarragon (picked)

Braised Rabbit And Mozzarella

2 bottles ale
200g salt
1 carrot (sliced)
2 sticks celery (cut into 2½cm pieces)
½ leek (sliced)
1 onion (chopped)
3 cloves garlic (chopped)
3 sprigs thyme, 2 bay leaves
1 bottle dry white wine
2½ litres chicken stock
3 large mozzarella balls (thinly sliced)
4 sheets spring roll pastry
2 potatoes (cut into potato strings - you will need a *mandolin* for this)

Garnish

4 hand-dived scallops
4 tomatoes (*blanched*, skin removed)
4 quail eggs

terrine mould (lined with cling film)

Method

For The Sweet And Sour Mustard Dressing

Simmer the vinegar with the grated horseradish, thyme, bay leaf, sugar and chillies for approximately 5 minutes. Leave to infuse and when cool, pass through a fine *chinois*. Bring the vinegar back to the boil and whisk in the turmeric and cornflour. Simmer for 5 minutes. Allow the liquid to cool before adding the Dijon mustard.

For The Tarragon Purée

Boil the tarragon leaves in salted water, then blend with a little of the water until it resembles the consistency of paint.

For The Braised Rabbit And Mozzarella (Allow up to 48 hours)

Boil the ale and salt together until the salt has dissolved, then allow to cool for 1 hour. Pour the ale over the rabbits and refrigerate overnight. This cures the rabbit and will add great flavour.

Wrap the rabbits in tin foil, or place in a pan with a tightly fitting lid. Cook in the oven for 1 hour at 160°C.

Dry the rabbits with a cloth. Roast in a pan to colour the skin golden brown, then leave to rest. In the same pan, *sauté* the vegetables until golden, then pour over the white wine and reduce by a third. Add the stock, then simmer.

Remove from the oven and leave to rest in the stock, then thoroughly remove all bones.

In the mould, alternately fill with a layer of rabbit meat, then a layer of mozzarella until the mix is all used up. Press and refrigerate for 12 hours, or overnight, until firm. Cut the rabbit 'terrine' into thick 2.5cm x 7.5cm pieces and wrap in the spring roll pastry, then finally wrap thoroughly in potato string.

Deep fry (190°C) for 2-3 minutes until crispy and golden.

The stock from the rabbit can be turned into rabbit jelly by passing it through muslin, then warming it up with gelatine (400ml to 4 leaves). Set in a tray until cold.

> **Chef's Tip**
> After cooking, leave the rabbit in the braising liquid to cool before picking. This keeps the meat from drying out.

To Serve

Serve the dish with a scallop roasted in olive oil and butter, dress with the tarragon purée and mustard sauce. Perhaps add a poached quail egg and some tomato.

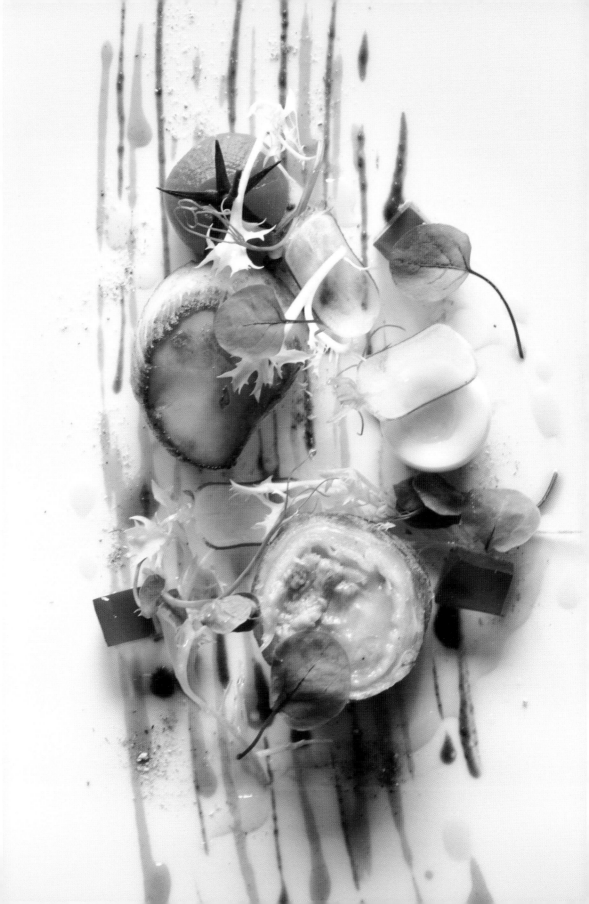

LINE CAUGHT SEA BASS 'FORESTIERE'

SERVES 4

Weiler Schlipf 'CS' Spätburgunder, Baden, Weingut
Claus Schneider (Germany)

Ingredients

Sea Bass

1 x 1-1½kg line caught sea bass
(filleted, pin boned)
50ml olive oil
50g unsalted butter
1 lemon (cut in half)

Vegetables

selection of young vegetables:
English onions
chervil roots
young carrots
young turnips
salsify
artichokes
tenderstem broccoli
cep mushrooms

Cabbage

1 Savoy cabbage
100ml double cream

Red Wine Sauce

250g shallots (peeled, chopped)
2 cloves garlic (crushed)
2 sprigs thyme
1 bay leaf
100ml red wine vinegar
500ml port
1 litre red wine
200g button mushrooms (sliced)
3 litres chicken stock
100ml veal glace
50ml olive oil

Method

For The Sea Bass

Preheat a good quality frying pan, add the olive oil, then place the fish skin down, gently pushing flat with a spatula to avoid the fish curling. Cook until the skin crisps, then add the butter, lowering the heat a little so it doesn't burn. When the fish has visibly cooked half way through, flip it over and squeeze a little lemon juice into the pan and over the fillet, then baste for a few seconds. Remove from the pan and rest before serving.

> **Chef's Tip**
>
> Leave the sea bass fillet a little undercooked in the centre and rest for a few minutes in a warm place. This will help the flesh taste creamy and sweet, not dry.

For The Vegetables

All the vegetables should be cooked gently from cold water or stock, up to the simmer, then refresh under cold running water, or simply rest on a tray. You may wish to reheat in olive oil and finish with butter in the same fashion as the fish.

For The Cabbage

Remove the leaves one by one and cut out the thick veins, slicing into fine pieces (*chiffonade*). Boil all of the cabbage in salty water to retain the vitamins and colour, then refresh under cold running water and dry on a cloth. Reduce the double cream until it thickens, then incorporate the cabbage.

For The Red Wine Sauce

Sweat the shallots with olive oil, thyme, garlic and bay leaf. Add the red wine vinegar and reduce until completely dry, then add the port and reduce until a syrup consistency.

Add the red wine and mushrooms, then reduce by two thirds. Finally, add the chicken stock and veal glace and simmer for approximately 2 hours. Strain through a fine *chinois* and reduce to a sauce consistency, about half a litre.

To Serve

Serve as pictured. A *reduction* of port or red wine can be added to freshen the sauce.

THACKERAY'S BLACK FOREST

SERVES 6

 Ice Wine, Black Diamond Label, Chateau Changyu Icewine Co (Liaoning, China)

Ingredients

Chocolate Crémeux
100ml whipping cream
100ml semi-skimmed milk
50g fresh egg yolks (2-3 eggs)
25g sugar
50g 70% dark chocolate

Cherry Gel
200g good quality cherry purée
20g sugar
2g agar agar

Kirsch Parfait
100g sugar
50ml water
3 leaves bronze gelatine (softened in cold water)
150g fresh egg yolks (7-8 eggs)
300ml double cream (whipped)
25ml good quality Kirsch

Marshmallow Dome
190g fresh egg whites (approximately 5 eggs)
350g sugar
100ml water
3 leaves bronze gelatine (softened in cold water)

Wild Sorrel Sponge
4 eggs
100g sugar
125g plain flour
4 tsp bitter lime powder
½ tsp green food colouring
6 tsp wild sorrel purée

Garnish
edible viola flowers
wood sorrel cress
fresh cherries (stoned)

6 *dariole* moulds (7cm)
6 metal dome moulds (8cm)
20cm square cake tin (greased, lined with parchment)

Method

For The Chocolate Crémeux
In a heavy bottomed saucepan, bring the milk and cream to the boil. Lightly whisk the sugar into the yolks. Pour a little of the milk mixture over the yolks and pour the rest back into the pan. Cook the mix to 85°C, whisking continuously. Pour the mix over the chocolate and whisk until dissolved. Pass through a fine sieve into a suitable container, then set in the fridge for 2 hours.

For The Cherry Gel
Bring the purée and sugar to the boil in a heavy bottomed pan. Whisk in the agar agar and boil again for 2-3 minutes. Pour into a container and set in the fridge for about 3 hours until solid. Blitz in a food processor with a little water until it reaches a gel consistency. Pass through a fine sieve into a sauce bottle. Reserve in the fridge.

For The Kirsch Parfait (Make the day before)
Whisk the egg yolks to a light ribbon stage. Mix the sugar and water, then bring to the boil in a small saucepan. Continue to boil and, using a food thermometer, take the temperature to 121°C. Add the soaked gelatine leaves to the hot sugar syrup. Mix thoroughly and slowly pour onto the egg yolks whilst still whisking. Continue whisking until it cools.
Fold in the whipped cream and Kirsch, then spoon into the *dariole* moulds and freeze overnight. Serve frozen.

For The Marshmallow Dome
Whisk the egg whites to a soft peak. Mix the sugar and water together, then bring to the boil in a small saucepan. Continue to boil up to 121°C, using a sugar thermometer to check. Add the softened gelatine to the hot sugar syrup. Mix thoroughly and slowly pour onto the egg whites whilst still whisking. Continue whisking until cool in temperature. Using a palette knife, fill the metal dome moulds and reserve in the fridge.

For The Wild Sorrel Sponge
Preheat the oven to 160°C.
Whisk the eggs and sugar until it reaches a thick ribbon stage. Fold in the flour, bitter lime powder, colouring and sorrel purée. Using a palette knife, spread into the prepared cake tin. Bake for 15 minutes until it is spongy throughout and a knife comes out clean from the middle. Leave to cool. Serve at room temperature.

To Serve
Using a palette knife, spread the chocolate crémeux down the middle of an oiled olive board. Tear the sorrel sponge and place around the edges of the crémeux swipe. Decorate with a few dots of the cherry gel. Place the Kirsch parfait upside down in the middle of the board. Carefully turn out the marshmallow dome and position directly on top of the parfait. Toast the dome using a blow torch. Garnish the dish with edible viola flowers, wood sorrel cress and fresh cherries.

FOOD & WINE PAIRING
BY BLUEBELL VINEYARD ESTATES

Located between the famous Bluebell Steam Railway and the historic Sheffield Park and Garden, the multi award-winning Bluebell Vineyard has been producing quality English Sparkling Wines, handmade by the traditional method, for almost a decade.

Planted in 2005, the vineyard's favoured climate and terroir ensures that it is able to rival the achievements of well-established wineries from around the world. By achieving over 25 national and international awards (including medals from Decanter and the IWC), Bluebell has confirmed its status amongst England's top producers.

Most recently, the vineyard was awarded the top mark for a Rosé at the prestigious 'Judgement of Parsons Green' for their Brut Rosé 2010, and was also the biggest medal winners at the English and Welsh Wine of the Year Competition 2014 (UKVA), notably taking a coveted Gold medal for its Classic Cuvée 2010. Jancis Robinson also awarded both the Brut Rosé 2010 and the Blanc de Blancs 2009 an impressive score of 17.5.

As the demand for English Sparkling Wine rapidly increases, the vineyard has quickly grown in size to almost 100 acres, stretching across two counties - East and West Sussex. Headed by winemaker, Kevin Sutherland, the team of Viticulturalists lovingly nurture the three classic Champagne grapes; Chardonnay, Pinot Noir and Pinot Meunier (as well as a small planting of Seyval Blanc) throughout the year and with the approach of harvest, the grapes are tasted daily to determine the optimum moment for hand harvesting.

Why not visit the vineyard for a tour and tasting and find out why its quality English Sparkling is receiving international acclaim. Visiting the vineyard couldn't be easier - take advantage of the rich Sussex heritage by travelling from London to East Grinstead station and boarding a Bluebell Railway Steam engine to the Sheffield Park Station, just minutes from the vineyard.

Food And Wine Pairing

For Fish

Bluebell Vineyard Hindleap Blanc De Blancs
A wine created exclusively from the noble Chardonnay grape. Our Blanc de Blanc is made from 100% Chardonnay grapes grown in our own vineyards. This wine has undergone an extended autolysis (aging on lees) for 30 months resulting in a more complex, sophisticated and 'Champagne' style wine. Released in March 2014, this wine has proved to be a big success and recently received a Decanter award. Aromas of peaches and lemon prevail, with fresh lemon/lime, wild honey and brioche flavours. Perfect with scallops, smoked salmon, caviar, Dover Sole, or as an aperitif. Also matches well with chicken and pork dishes.

For Dessert

Bluebell Vineyard Hindleap Brut Rosé
A consistent award-winner, Bluebell's Brut Rosé is a blend of vintage Pinot Noir and Pinot Meunier, aged for a minimum of 18 months. Pale pink in the glass with exuberant mousse, the flavours are often compared to strawberries and cream. Hints of rose petal, cranberry and zingy freshness mean this wine matches perfectly with strawberries and cream, soufflé, vanilla cheesecake and even scones and jam. Also enjoy with blinis, lobster, scallops, smoked and poached salmon to begin your meal in style.

For Meat

Bluebell Vineyard Hindleap Classic Cuvée
The Classic Cuvée is produced from all three classic Champagne varieties; Chardonnay, Pinot Noir and Pinot Meunier. Following the liqueur de tirage, the wine is left to age on its lees for a minimum of 30 months to give body and impart character and toasty flavours.

This wine is golden in colour with creamy effervescence. Biscuit and apple aromas are evident on the nose with hints of mango and baked pear on the palate. A true Classic. Our Classic works beautifully with game, calamari, monkfish, fish and chips and soft cheeses.

Bluebell Vineyard Estates, Glenmore Farm, Sliders Lane, Furners Green, East Sussex, TN22 3RU.
T: 01825 791 561 www.bluebellvineyard.co.uk

SOUTH EAST LARDER

Introduction by Stephen Crane, Head Chef, Ockenden Manor Hotel & Spa

The South East is a region full of rich pickings for chefs to create wonderful dishes. Food miles are low because there is a wealth of great local producers - some of whom are highlighted here as suppliers to restaurants featured in this beautiful book. I am Sussex born and bred and I live in Balcombe which is next to Cuckfield. I have worked at Ockenden Manor since 2001 and we won our first Michelin star in 2004 which we have retained every year and this is something the team and I are immensely proud of. Undoubtedly one of the key components of our success is that we use quality, locally sourced ingredients on our menu. We have great relationships with local suppliers, some of whom we have been working with for many years. They know exactly what we want and they deliver excellent produce to us every time and this ensures that the high standards we set are continuously delivered - it is a team effort, from field (or sea) to fork!

The landscape in Sussex and the wider South East region is not only some of the most beautiful in the country but also some of the richest and most abundant. Grapes grown here are made into award-winning English sparkling wines, fresh fish and shellfish are landed daily at Hastings and Newhaven, free-range game is sustainably harvested from the Balcombe Estate, the Trenchmore Sussex beef from the 12th Century farm are slow grown, the Southdown lambs from the Goodwood Estate have flourished on the Downs for hundreds of years and their Dairy Shorthorn produce deliciously rich and organic Goodwood milk and cream, some of which is then made into a range of traditional hand-made cheeses in Goodwood's own Cheese room. We are very lucky to be based in the South East and have all this on our doorstep. We use these ingredients and many others from the region on our menu which mixes innovation and tradition, echoing the atmosphere of the hotel.

218
SOUTH EAST LARDER

MEAT

BALCOMBE ESTATE FINE GAME
Bowders Farm, Balcombe, West Sussex, RH17 6QH
T: 07824 366 758 or 07780 119 163
www.balcombefinegame.co.uk

Balcombe Fine Game is locally sourced and is completely free-range. Bowders Farm supply venison, rabbit, pheasant, duck, partridge, pigeon, quail, guinea fowl, turkey, goose and various speciality game sausages.

CHART FARM
Seal Chart, Sevenoaks, Kent, TN15 0ES
T: 01732 761 672   www.chartfarm.com

A family-run business producing top quality venison for over 30 years on their farm in Kent. The deer, mostly Fallow and Sika, are raised on 400 acres of pasture and woodland. There is also a wonderful butchers shop selling top quality, dry aged beef and a host of other top end cuts.

COURT FARM BUTCHERY AND COUNTRY LARDER
Upper Halling, Rochester, Kent, ME2 1HR
T: 01634 240 547   www.courtfarm.org

The Lingham family have been farming Court Farm since 1871. Specialising in naturally reared beef and lamb, in 2003 they opened the Butchery and Country Larder farm shop, providing a wide range of home produced and locally sourced produce.

GOODWOOD HOME FARM
Chichester, West Sussex, PO18 0QF
T: 01243 755 153
www.goodwood.com/goodwood-home-farm

Goodwood Home Farm raise rare and native breeds, some indigenous to the Estate, offering unique tasting meats and dairy products.

JOHN MURRAY BUTCHER AND GAME DEALER
Unit 3-4, The Parade, Loxwood, West Sussex, RH14 0SB
T: 01403 752 859

John Murray Butcher and Game Dealer, offers a tasty and healthy alternative to lamb, chicken, beef or pork and is dedicated to promoting healthy, wild and delicious British game meat.

THE FARMERS BUTCHER
Swallowfields Farm, Blackhill Road, Bramshaw
T: 01794 523 323

The Farmers Butcher supplies New Forest Marque pork and beef. All animals are reared on the farm - they also have a licence for wild boar.

THE SUSSEX LARDER
7b St Marys Walk, Hailsham, BN27 1AF
T: 01323 442 031
www.sussexlarder.co.uk

A local family run butchers in Hailsham offering quality meat, often at supermarket prices. For over 20 years, they have been serving up beautiful meat to the community that not only looks great but also tastes great too.

TRENCHMORE FARM
Burnthouse Lane, Horsham, RH13 8DG
T: 07711 698 279
www.trenchmore.co.uk

Trenchmore Farm produces local dry-aged beef and supplies to gastro pubs and restaurants. Their breeds include Sussex, Red Wagyu and Red Aberdeen Angus. All meat is dry-aged for a minimum of 28 days, ensuring fantastic quality beef.

FISH

PH FISH
3-4 Rock-A-Nore Road, Hastings, TN34 3DW
T: 01424 444 965

Paul Hodges of PH Fish has over 30 years experience in the fishing industry. He is one of the few suppliers certified under the Marine Stewardship Council - carrying this accreditation for sustainable fish. Paul also manages Hastings Fish Market and has established his own smokery.

BRIGHTON AND NEWHAVEN FISH SALES (BNFS)
South Quay, Basin Road South, Aldrington Basin, Brighton, East Sussex, BN41 1WF
T: 01273 420 123
www.brighton-fish-sales.co.uk

Brighton and Newhaven Fish Sales provide fish and shellfish of the highest quality and freshness.

DAIRY & EGGS

FLUFFETTS FREE-RANGE EGGS
Hockeys Farm, South Gorley, Fordingbridge, Hampshire, SP6 2PW
T: 01425 489 028   www.fluffettsfarm.co.uk

Fluffetts have established a reputation locally for producing and distributing the finest quality eggs and are committed exclusively to the free-range sector.

HIGH WEALD DAIRY
Temains Farm, Horsted Keynes, West Sussex, RH17 7EA
T: 01825 791 636   www.highwealddairy.co.uk

A family run cheese dairy. Award-winning British cheeses made from cow, sheep and goat milk. Cheeses are available to buy online, at local delicatessens, farm shops and independent food outlets.

LYBURN FARMHOUSE CHEESEMAKERS
Lyburn Farm, Landford, Salisbury, SP5 2DN
T: 01794 399 982   www.lyburncheese.co.uk

Producers of different handmade cheeses, made from their own pasteurised cows milk and a vegetarian rennet.

SPECIALITY FOODS

LODSWORTH LARDER
The Street, Lodsworth, Petworth, West Sussex, GU28 9BZ
T: 01798 86 1947   www.lodsworthlarder.com

Lodsworth Larder is a community run, eco friendly, village shop, situated in the heart of the Southdowns National Park. It sells a wide variety of fresh produce and groceries.

MEDITERIA
Unit 4a, The Lansbury Estate, 102 Lower Guildford Road, Woking, Surrey, GU21 2EP
T: 08458 844 500   www.mediteria.com

Mediteria is a market leading importer and distributor of the finest Spanish food products in the UK. It provides premium products and services to trade only clients, such as delicatessens, caterers, hotels and restaurants.

WINES

BOLNEY WINE ESTATE
Foxhole Lane, Bolney, Haywards Heath, RH17 5NB
T: 01444 881 575   www.bolneywineestate.com

Bolney Wine Estate began back in 1972 as Bookers Vineyard with just three acres of vines. Over time it has expanded to 39 acres and is now an award-winning specialist wine maker of top quality red, white and traditional method sparkling wines.

RIDGEVIEW WINE ESTATE
Fragbarrow Lane, Ditchling Common, Sussex, BN6 8TP
T: 0845 345 7292   www.ridgeview.co.uk

Ridgeview was founded in1994 by Mike and Chris Roberts and is dedicated to creating world class sparkling wines in the South Downs of England. Their vineyards specialise in growing classic grape varieties to make the highest quality, bottle fermented sparkling wines.

GLOSSARY

AL DENTE

Al dente describes vegetables that are cooked to the 'tender crisp' phase - still offering resistance to the bite, but cooked through. Al dente can also describe cooked pasta which is firm but not hard.

BAIN-MARIE

A pan or other container of hot water with a bowl placed on top of it. This allows the steam from the water to heat the bowl so ingredients can be gently heated or melted.

BEURRE BLANC

French translates as 'white butter'. A hot emulsified butter sauce made with a reduction of vinegar and/or white wine (normally Muscadet) and grey shallots. Cold, whole butter is blended off the heat to prevent separation.

BEURRE NOISETTE

Unsalted butter is melted over a low heat until it begins to caramelise and brown. When it turns a nutty colour, it should be removed from the heat to stop it burning. Can be used as a base for butter sauces or added to cakes and batters.

BLANCH

Boiling an ingredient before removing it and plunging it in ice cold water in order to stop the cooking process.

BRUNOISE

A type of culinary cut in which food is diced into 3.175mm cubes. The formal-looking little squares add colour and elegance to dishes.

CARTOUCHE

A piece of greaseproof paper that covers the surface of a stew, soup, stock or sauce to reduce evaporation.

CHIFFONADE

A chopping technique in which herbs or leafy green vegetables (such as spinach and basil) are cut into long, thin strips.

CHINOIS

A conical sieve with an extremely fine mesh. It is used to strain custards, purées, soups and sauces, producing a very smooth texture.

CLARIFIED BUTTER

Milk fat rendered from butter to separate the milk solids and water from the butter fat.

CONCASSE

To roughly chop any ingredient, usually vegetables, most specifically applied to tomatoes, with tomato concasse being a tomato that has been peeled and seeded (seeds and skins removed).

CONFIT

A method of cooking where the meat is cooked and submerged in a liquid to add flavour. Often this liquid is rendered fat. Confit can also apply to fruits - fruit confits are cooked and preserved in sugar, the result is like candied fruits.

CREPINETTE

Crépine is the French word for 'pig's caul' in which a crépinette is wrapped instead of a casing.

DARIOLE

A French term that refers to small, cylinder shaped moulds.

DEGLAZE

A fancy term for using the flavour-packed brown bits stuck to the bottom of a pan to make a sauce or gravy.

EMULSION/EMULSIFY

In the culinary arts, an emulsion is a mixture of two liquids that would ordinarily not mix together, like oil and vinegar.

FLAMBE

A cooking procedure in which alcohol is added to a hot pan to create a burst of flames.

FRENCH TRIMMED

French trimmed is a decorative preparation method done to meat, so that a bone protrudes from it. Often fancy paper frills are placed on the bone for serving aesthetics.

To French trim, fat, meat or skin is cut away to expose a piece of bone, so that it sticks out.

It also means that any excess fat is cut off. French Trimming can be done to lamb chops and bigger cuts; it can even can be done to chicken legs or breasts.

ITALIAN MERINGUE

Italian meringue is made by beating egg whites until they reach soft, fluffy peaks, then slowly streaming in boiling sugar and beating the mixture until it is thick and glossy.

JULIENNE

A culinary knife cut in which the vegetable is cut into long thin strips, similar to matchsticks.

JUS LIE/JUS

Jus lié refers to meat juice (jus) that has been reduced by heat. It can also be lightly thickened with either arrowroot starch or corn starch.

LIQUOR

The liquid that is left over from the cooking of meat or vegetables. Can be incorporated into sauces and gravy.

MACERATED

Raw, dried, or preserved fruit and vegetables soaked in a liquid to soften the food or to absorb the flavour.

MAILLARD REACTION

The Maillard reaction is a chemical reaction between amino acids and reducing sugars that gives browned foods their desirable flavour. It is sometimes called 'browning' but helps improve flavour significantly.

MANDOLIN

A cooking utensil used for slicing and for cutting juliennes. Slices can be very thin, and be made very quickly. It ensures that all slices are uniform.

MIREPOIX

Finely diced combination of celery (pascal, celery or celeriac), onions and carrots. There are many regional mirepoix variations, which can sometimes be just one of these ingredients, or include additional spices creating a rich, flavoursome base to sauces or stews.

MONTE

To emulsify with butter, usually used to finish a sauce.

NEW YORK DRESSED

This refers to poultry. The bird has been slaughtered and plucked, with the head and feet left intact.

PANNE

To coat with flour, beaten egg and breadcrumbs for deep frying.

PATE A BOMBE

A pâte à bombe is the French term for a mixture used as a base for making chocolate mousse and other mousse-like desserts.

QUENELLE

A finely minced fish or meat mixture formed into small portions, poached in stock and served in a sauce, or as a garnish to other dishes. The term is also used to describe their characteristic shape - a neat, three-sided oval (resembling a mini rugby ball) that is formed by gently smoothing the mixture between two dessert spoons. A quenelle shape can also be formed from other foods such as chocolate mousse.

REDUCTION

The process of thickening a liquid in order to intensify the flavour. This is done by evaporating the moisture in a liquid.

SABAYON

Made by beating egg yolks with a liquid over simmering water until thickened and increased in volume. The liquid can be water, but Champagne or wine is often used.

SAUTE

To fry in a small amount of fat.

SEEDING/TEMPERED (CHOCOLATE)

'Tempering is like organising individual dancers at a party into a Conga line. For chocolate, temperature and motion are the party organisers that bring all the individual dancing crystals of fatty acids together in long lines and, in the process, create a stable crystallisation throughout the chocolate mass'. Chocomap.com

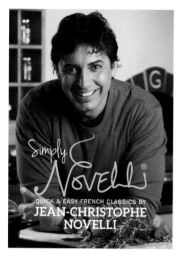

Simply **Novelli** ®

QUICK & EASY FRENCH CLASSICS BY
JEAN-CHRISTOPHE NOVELLI

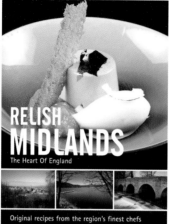

RELISH MIDLANDS
The Heart Of England

Original recipes from the region's finest chefs
Introduction by Andreas Antona

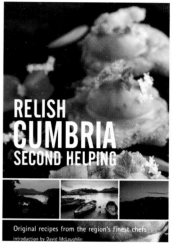

RELISH CUMBRIA SECOND HELPING

Original recipes from the region's finest chefs
Introduction by David McLaughlin

Relish **SCOTLAND SECOND HELPING**

Original recipes from Scotland's finest chefs
and restaurants. Introduction by Tom Kitchin

Relish **COTSWOLDS & OXFORDSHIRE**

Original recipes from the Cotswolds and
Oxfordshire's finest chefs and restaurants

OVER 100 RECIPES

Relish **NORTH EAST & YORKSHIRE**

Original recipes from the North East
and Yorkshire's finest chefs and
restaurants. Introduction by celebrity chefs
James Martin and Hairy Biker, Si King.

Relish **SOUTH WEST**

Original recipes from the South West's
finest chefs and restaurants.
Introduction by Michael Caines MBE.

Relish **WALES SECOND HELPING**

Original recipes from the region's
finest chefs and restaurants.
Introduction by James Sommerin.

Relish **NORTH WEST**

Original recipes from the region's
finest chefs and restaurants.
Introduction by Paul Heathcote, MBE.

BEST OF BRITISH

Relish Publications is an independent publishing house offering an exclusive insight into Britain's finest restaurants and chefs through their series of award-winning recipe books.

Each book contains signature recipes from your favourite chefs, recommended wines, stunning food photography and an impressive guide to each participating restaurant, plus a larder featuring the region's best produce suppliers. These ingredients make the Relish series an ultimate 'foodies' guide for individuals wishing to dine in great restaurants or create outstanding recipes at home.

The series of beautiful hard back recipe books is available to buy in the featured restaurants, all good bookshops and online at the Relish bookshop or on Amazon.

For more information please visit **www.relishpublications.co.uk**

Duncan and Teresa Peters founded Relish Publications in 2009, through a passion for good food, a love of publishing and after recognising the need to promote the fantastic chefs and restaurants each region in the UK has to offer.
Relish Publications also specialise in bespoke cookbooks for individual chefs.

Since launching, their goal was simple. Create beautiful books with high quality contributors (each edition features a selection of the region's top chefs) to build a unique and invaluable recipe book.

As recipe book specialists, their team works with hundreds of chefs personally to ensure each edition exceeds the readers' expectations.

Thank you for Relishing with us!

HERE'S WHAT SOME OF BRITAIN'S BEST CHEFS HAVE SAID ABOUT WORKING WITH RELISH

"The Relish team has truly been amazing to work with. To have produced my book within two months from start to finish, only shows how professional a team of people can be." *Jean-Christophe Novelli*

"The Relish cookbook offers the home cook some great inspiration to make the most of these wonderful ingredients in season." *Tom Kitchin, The Kitchin, Edinburgh*

"With mouth-watering, easy to follow recipes and beautiful photography, this book is a must have for any foodie, from professional chef to the inspired home cook." *Michael Caines MBE*

"Relish brings together some of the most talented chefs from the regions. It shines the spotlight on the exceptional ways in which fresh, seasonal, local ingredients are put to good use." *Gary Jones, Executive Head Chef, Le Manoir aux Quat'Saisons*

"Relish Wales Second Helping has been lovingly created and showcases the very best of our beautiful land. Great chefs, great food and sumptuous dishes. It makes for essential reading and I'm proud to be part of it." *James Sommerin*

"I feel very proud to be championing the Relish Scotland book. The chefs and restaurants featured, use the natural ingredients with an instinctive understanding of how to make the best of what's in season." *Nick Nairn*

LOOKING TO DINE IN THE UK'S FINEST RESTAURANTS?

Visit the Relish Restaurant Guide to find the very best your region has to offer.

The Relish team has worked with all of the chefs listed on the Relish website and we have visited every highly recommended and acclaimed restaurant. This recipe makes the **Relish Restaurant Guide** genuine and unique.

If you would like to be taken on an epic journey to the finest restaurants in each region, to download more mouth-watering recipes, to join our exclusive Relish Rewards club, or to add to your collection of Relish books, visit **www.relishpublications.co.uk**

DOWNLOAD YOUR FREE SAMPLE APP TODAY

All of our regional cookbooks are now available to download and purchase.

Browse hundreds of recipes with beautiful photography and easy to follow instructions from a selection of the UK's finest chefs and restaurants.

 Download your FREE sample pages now from the App Store/Relish Cookbook.

Apple, the Apple logo and iPhone are trademarks of Apple Inc, registered in the US and other countries, App Store is a service mark of Apple Inc.

HINTS & TIPS...

HOW TO MAKE ICE CREAM WITHOUT A MACHINE

Although relatively inexpensive these days, not everyone has access to an ice cream machine. That's no reason not to follow some of these delicious recipes found in the Relish South East book. Although more time consuming than a machine, excellent results can be obtained by following this simple method.

Follow the recipe right up until it tells you to churn in the machine, including any chilling time in the fridge.

Take your mixture from the fridge and stir with a rubber spatula. Transfer it to a suitable plastic container with a lid. There should be at least 2cm space at the top to allow the mixture to expand when freezing. Cover and place in the freezer for two hours.

Remove from the freezer and beat with a hand mixer, still in the container, to break up the ice crystals that are beginning to form. Cover and return to the freezer for a further 2 hours. (If you don't have a hand mixer then you may use a fork and some 'elbow grease' to break up the crystals).

Remove from the freezer and beat again with the hand mixer. The ice cream should be thickening up nicely at this point but too soft to scoop. Return it to the freezer for an additional hour. Beat again. If your ice cream is still not thickened sufficiently, repeat this process again after another hour. When the ice cream has thickened properly, stir in any add-ins at this point (honeycomb, nuts...). Do not beat with the hand mixer after the add-ins have been mixed in.

Place the tightly sealed container in the freezer and allow the ice cream to freeze until firm. The ice cream should be removed from the freezer 15-20 minutes before you wish to eat it. This will make scooping easier.

This method will also work for sorbets. Sometimes sorbets may go a bit 'icy' or 'crumbly' if left for too long in the freezer. This can be rectified by blitzing in a food processor just before serving.

HOW TO MAKE A SUGAR STOCK SYRUP

This makes about 750ml sugar stock. It can be stored in a sterilised jar in the fridge for a couple of months.

500g white sugar
500ml water

Place the sugar and water in a pan. Dissolve slowly over a very low heat. You must not allow the syrup to boil until all the sugar has dissolved, about 5 minutes. Once completely dissolved, bring to the boil, then simmer for 5 minutes.

CONVERSION CHART

COOKING TEMPERATURES

Degrees Celsius	Fahrenheit	Gas Mark
140	275	1
150	300	2
160–170	325	3
180	350	4
190	375	5
200–210	400	6
220	425	7
230	450	8
240	475	9

*Temperatures for fan-assisted ovens are, as a general rule, normally about 20°C lower than regular oven temperature.

WEIGHT MEASUREMENT CONVERSIONS

1 teaspoon (5ml/5g)	$^1/_4$ oz
1 tablespoon (15ml/15g)	$^3/_4$ oz
10g	$^1/_2$ oz
25g	1oz
50g	2oz
75g	3oz
150g	5oz
200g	7oz
250g	9oz
350g	12oz
450g	1lb
1kg	2.2lb

VOLUME MEASUREMENT CONVERSIONS

55ml	2 fl oz
150ml	$^1/_4$ pt
275ml	$^1/_2$ pint
570ml	1 pt
1 litre	$1^3/_4$ pt